Workbook

How to Get Your
Prayers
Answered

Your 10-Day Spiritual Action Plan

KENNETH
COPELAND
PUBLICATIONS

by Kenneth and Gloria
Copeland

How to Get Your Prayers Answered: Your 10-Day Spiritual Action Plan

ISBN 978-1-60463-104-3   30-3030

16 15 14 13 12 11   6 5 4 3 2 1

© 2011 Eagle Mountain International Church Inc. aka Kenneth Copeland Ministries

For more information about Kenneth Copeland Ministries, call 800-600-7395 or visit www.kcm.org.

CD Credits:

Executive Producers | Kenneth & Gloria Copeland

Produced by | Robert Wirtz for Eagle Mountain Productions

Additional Production by | Michael Howell

Engineered by | Robert Wirtz & Michael Howell

Mixed & Mastered by | Robert Wirtz

Production Assistance | Christen McCarley

Recorded and Mixed at | Eagle Mountain Recording Studios, Newark, Texas | Front Room Studios, Keller, Texas | Michael Howell Recording Studio, Murrieta, California

Musicians: Acoustic Guitar | Michael Howell | Keyboards | Melissa Spangler
Additional Keyboards & Programming | Robert Wirtz & Michael Howell

Vocalists: Jeff Spangler, Melissa Spangler & Avery Spangler

Table of
Contents

How to Use
Your LifeLine Kit

How to Use
Your LifeLine Kit

We believe this *10-Day Spiritual Action Plan for How to Get Your Prayers Answered* will change the way you live. As you invite God into every part of your life, not only will you become increasingly aware of your living contact with Him, but you will also see Him move on your behalf because of your partnership with Him. To accomplish this, we've created one of the most in-depth resources Kenneth Copeland Ministries has ever made available on this subject—all in one place. Here are some practical tips to get you started and help you make the most of this kit:

- Commit to making the next 10 days your days for renewing your mind. Set aside any distractions and be prepared to make adjustments in your life so you can get the most out of this kit.
- This plan should be a blessing, not a burden. If you miss a day or can't quite get through one day's materials, just start where you left off at your next opportunity. If you have to, be flexible with the kit to ensure you make it to the end. If you only have half an hour a day, that's fine—commit that! It may take longer to complete the kit, but you can be confident those days will still be some of the most life-changing days you've ever had.
- Use this LifeLine workbook as your starting point each day, to guide your reading, listening, watching and journaling. Before you know it, you'll be saturating your life with God's WORD like never before.
- We recommend that you:

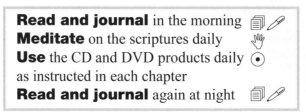

Read and journal in the morning
Meditate on the scriptures daily
Use the CD and DVD products daily
as instructed in each chapter
Read and journal again at night

Remember, the goal is to do a little every day. Steady doses are the best medicine.

- This is an action book! Have a pen handy to underline and take notes.
- Fully engage with all the materials. Write in your workbook, speak the scriptures, pray the prayers, sing with the music and take time to enjoy the materials in every way.
- Carry your daily action card and refer to it throughout your day as a connecting point with God.
- Make your study time focused. Do your best to remove distractions and find a quiet place.

You are closer than ever to developing an effective prayer life and getting your prayers answered! God loves you and He is *for* you. We're standing with you, and remember that "Jesus Is Lord!"

Chapter One
The Call to Prayer

Today, you'll discover:

What prayer is

What role prayer plays in your fellowship with other believers

How you know you can go "boldly unto the throne of grace"

How a habit can become an addiction

Steps to making prayer a priority in your life.

The Aim of Prayer
by Kenneth Copeland

Early in my ministry, I learned a vital lesson: For any effort to be successful, it must be backed by prayer. Effective praying is the key to success in every area of life.

Your aim in prayer is to be effective. Jesus is the perfect example of One who knows how to pray and get results. He spent hours separated from people, praying and fellowshiping with His heavenly Father. The time He spent in prayer prepared Him to minister effectively.

As a believer, you can achieve the same results Jesus did during His earthly ministry—and more. Jesus said, "He that believeth on me, the works that I do shall he do also; and greater works than these shall he do; because I go unto my Father" (John 14:12). These "greater works" can be accomplished today, but only by believers who have a deep, sincere prayer life with God.

This LifeLine kit is designed to strengthen your relationship with God through an awareness of the importance of prayer. With a solid foundation from The WORD of God, you will understand the basic principles of prayer: its purpose, how to pray and how to get results.

What Is Prayer?

As the foundation of every Christian endeavor, prayer plays a vital role in living a successful and fruitful Christian life. Time spent with God is vital to your success. Study the lives of the great men and women of God from the past, and you'll see the strong emphasis they placed on prayer. Without prayer, they never would have been able to achieve such tremendous results.

But what *is* prayer exactly?

Prayer is not an emotional release or an escape valve. It is much more than just asking God for a favor. Most important, prayer is not a religious exercise. God responds to faith, so just repetition and beautiful words do not get the ear of God. Jesus said in Matthew 6:7, "But when ye pray, use not vain repetitions, as the heathen do: for they think that they shall be heard for their much speaking."

Prayer is an attitude. It is communicating and fellowshiping with God. You can live in an attitude of prayer every moment, being in constant contact with your heavenly Father.

You may say, "But I can't spend all my time in prayer!" Yes, you can! In 1 Thessalonians 5:17, the Apostle Paul instructed the Church to "pray without ceasing." Luke 18:1 says, "Men ought always to pray, and not to faint."

The No. 1 priority in God's heart is to spend quality time with us daily. We need to be able to hear His voice and follow the promptings of His Holy Spirit. Living in continual fellowship with Him is possible every day for the believer.

THE BLESSING of Fellowship

The more time you spend in God's presence, the more you will act and think like Him. He has already given you His nature. Fruit bearing comes through prayer.

Jesus always separated Himself from people to spend time in prayer. Spending time with the Father in fellowship and prayer kept Him in tune with the Holy Spirit.

Fellowshiping with God will cause your desires, attitudes, actions and beliefs to line up with His. Then, when you pray, you will simply be voicing His will. The reality of God will burn into your consciousness. You will not be crying out to a God who is 92 million miles away. He will be right there—closer than a brother (Proverbs 18:24). As you draw nigh to God, He will draw nigh to you (James 4:8). No danger, no circumstance, no problem in this world can come near you with God Almighty by your side!

Fellowshiping with God will give birth to a deep, strong faith and trust in His ability. Your prayer life will take on new meaning.

Plus, prayer is vital for our fellowship with one another (Ephesians 4:14-16). Compare the Body of Christ to a brick building. The bricks would topple if they were not joined together. Mortar forms those bricks into a solid, impenetrable wall. It is held together, or made useful, by the effectual working of every part. In the same way, the power of love, through prayer and intercession, is the mortar which knits the Body of Christ together. Each member, or "brick," contributes his part by building up the Body and strengthening it through prayer. If one is injured or weakened in some way, the others are able to stand in prayer and make up for that weakness.

Boldly Before the Throne

In order to get results in prayer, you must be convinced that God wants to answer your prayers. In fact, He is as ready and willing to answer you as He was to answer Jesus during His earthly ministry. This may be difficult to believe, but it is true.

I remember how amazed I was to learn about God's willingness to answer my prayers because I had always thought of myself as unworthy. Why would God bother to answer *my* prayers? Ignorance of His WORD kept me from receiving His best in my life.

Once I realized the importance of The WORD of God, my attitude changed. I realized God does not see His children as unworthy. Notice how Jesus prayed: "...that the world may know that thou hast sent me, *and hast loved them, as thou hast loved me*" (John 17:23). Just think! God loves you and me as much as He loves Jesus! We *are* worthy!

Knowing God is ready to answer your prayers will make you serious about your prayer life. Because you are a child of God, you have an open invitation from Him to come into the throne room at any time.

Never take this prayer privilege lightly. You do not have to enter His presence crawling on your hands and knees. You can boldly stand before God without a sense of guilt, shame or condemnation. Hebrews 4:16 says, "Let us therefore come boldly unto the throne of grace, that we may obtain mercy, and find grace to help in time of need."

The Role of Faith

It pleases God to answer our prayers, but He can only manifest Himself in the earth through believers who are operating in faith. Faith makes prayer effective and it pleases God (Hebrews 11:6). However, there will be no strong faith without deep and intimate fellowship with the Father. This is the very heart of a successful prayer life.

Fellowship is the mother of faith because you can only put your faith and confidence in God to the extent you know Him. Just as in any relationship, spending time in fellowship with your heavenly Father is the only way to become personally acquainted with Him.

Not long after I became a Christian, I asked a minister to pray for me. I was expecting to hear a long, beautiful prayer—one that would cause people to fall on their knees in repentance before God! What I heard was just the opposite. He laid his hand on my chest, bowed his head, and said, "Lord, bless him. Meet his every need." He then turned and walked away. I was left standing there thinking, *How could he do that to me? I have big problems. It should have taken at least 20 minutes of hard praying to cover everything.*

The major difference separating that minister and me was the degree of faith at work in our lives. He was operating in faith, praying exactly what he meant. I was a baby Christian, looking for a physical manifestation of some kind.

The length of time or how hard you pray makes no difference. When you pray in faith, you have confidence in God's willingness to use His power to answer your prayer.

The man who has confidence in God is very difficult to defeat. He knows, regardless of what comes, he can pray and God will move in his behalf. The key then, to success in prayer, is expecting results. Many Christians think, *I'll pray and maybe something will happen.* They say, "I'm just hoping and praying."

If you are only hoping to get results, you will never receive from God. "Hoping to get" is not the same as "believing you receive." The promises of God bring hope in hopeless situations. However, hope has no substance by itself. "I hope to get healed someday." You hope to receive someday, but someday never comes. Faith brings hope into reality and gives it substance. Hebrews 11:1 says, "Now faith is the substance of things hoped for, the evidence of things not seen." The object of hope becomes a reality through faith. Hope is always in the future. Faith is always now.

Faith causes you to receive from God. The believer who is operating in faith believes God's power went to work the moment he prayed.

As a born-again believer, you have everything you need to succeed in this life. When you pray in faith and confidence, all of heaven's resources are at your disposal! Determine in your heart you will maintain consistent, intimate fellowship with God so your prayer life will be based on personal knowledge of Him. Then let your journey begin!

Today's Connection Points

⊙ **Worship CD: "Word of God Speak" (Track 1)**

Let The WORD of God speak to you today as you come before Him ready to receive.

⊙ **DVD: "Make Time" (Chapter 1)**

Make spending time in The WORD and in prayer the No. 1 priority in your life. Gloria explains how, as you do, you'll begin walking in God's fullness!

Faith in Action

✋ ***Forge an attitude of prayer in your life today.***
Commit to a regular prayer life, staying in continual contact with God.

Notes:

Make Prayer a Priority
by Gloria Copeland

If you have your ear turned toward God these days, I suspect you've heard Him say something to you about prayer. Maybe that's what prompted you to pick up this kit. He's been calling you to spend more time in prayer, to make it a higher priority in your life.

I know that's true because He's been telling me the same thing. In fact, the more people I talk to about it, the more convinced I am that God is calling all His people to prayer.

The reason is simple. These are the last of the last days. God is ready to move through us in magnificent and supernatural ways. But He can't do that if we're not walking in the spirit. He can't work through people who are so busy with the affairs of the flesh that they can't hear His voice.

He needs people who will pray—not just when they happen to think about it, but every day. He needs people who will build their whole lives around prayer and make it their No. 1 priority.

Have you ever noticed how Jesus operated when He was on the earth? He placed great importance on prayer. His prayer life was absolutely amazing. The night before He chose the 12 disciples, He was in prayer all night long!

Well, Jesus didn't do things one way and tell us to do something else. He expects us to follow His example.

First Thessalonians 5:17 tells us to "pray without ceasing." Ephesians 6:18 tells us to pray "always with all prayer and supplication in the Spirit." All through the New Testament we're told to pray! And now it's time for us to do our job. I don't mean just one or two of us—I mean the whole army of God.

Your natural human reaction to that call for prayer may be to say, "Hey, I hardly have time enough to handle all the crises in my life as it is now. I can't afford to spend any more time in prayer!" But, the truth is, you can't afford not to. You need to tap into what time spent with the Father can do for you.

It's when we begin to make prayer our priority—to lay aside the natural things, take up the things of God and walk in the power of the Spirit—that the glory of God will be reflected in us.

"Oh, Gloria," you say, "you just don't know how hectic my life is. I just can't do that!"

Yes, you can. It's just a matter of rearranging your priorities.

More Than Enough

Maybe you're like me. When I was first saved, no one had to urge me to put The WORD first place. No one had to tell me to turn off the television and put down the newspaper. I totally lost interest in those things because Ken and I had our lives in such bad shape that we were desperate for God. We were in trouble. We weren't on the bottom of the barrel. We were *under* the barrel!

We knew that The WORD of God was the only answer to our desperate situation. So it was easy for us to sell out to it and spend time in The WORD and in living contact with God day and night.

But after I'd walked with God for a while and things began to get comfortable, the desire I once had for The WORD began to wane.

Ken and I had paid our debts and we began enjoying THE BLESSING[1] of God. Before I knew it, I had begun to let too much of my time be taken up by other things. They weren't sinful things; they were just things I enjoyed doing. Almost without realizing it, my appetite for the things of God began to wane. Instead of hungering more for time with Him than for anything else, I found myself enjoying other activities and interests more. Those activities would have been fine had I kept them in the right place, but they occupied too much of my time and attention.

I hardly noticed it had happened until, one day in 1977, I was attending one of Kenneth E. Hagin's meetings and he began to prophesy. Part of that prophecy said to purpose in your heart that you will not be lazy, that you will not draw back, hold back or sit down, but that you will rise up, march forward and become on fire.

When I heard that, it dawned on me that I had let myself slip spiritually. I realized I'd become lazy about the things of God. I was still spending time in The WORD, but not as much as before, and I wasn't as full of zeal either. (That will always be the case. You can't be spiritually on fire without spending a sufficient amount of time with God.)

The LORD began to deal with me about it. I prayed and determined in my heart that I would change things. In order to simplify my life, I asked The LORD to show me what activities I should eliminate and what I should take on.

He led me to drop certain things out of my life that were stealing my time with Him. He also told me to do certain things that would help me get back in the habit of spending time with Him as I should.

One thing He led me to do was get up an hour earlier in the morning so I could spend time with Him before I began my day. When I started, it was winter. My alarm clock would go off and my flesh would say, *You don't want to get up. It's too dark! It's too cold!* My bed would feel so wonderful and warm that there were a

---

[1]The Lord instructed Ken to emphasize THE BLESSING by using all capital letters when referring to it, so I like to do that too.

few mornings during the first few weeks that I'd agree with my body and go back to sleep.

I didn't let that stop me though. If I became lazy and went back to sleep, I'd repent. Then I just asked God to help me, and the next morning I'd go at it again! Eventually, my body became trained.

Your body can be trained to follow God just as it can be trained to follow the devil. Hebrews 5:14 says that mature believers have their "senses and mental faculties...trained by practice to discriminate and distinguish between...good and...evil" *(The Amplified Bible)*. If you practice the things of God, your body will eventually begin to cooperate with you.

For me, getting up earlier was a challenge for a while. But eventually my body learned it wouldn't receive that extra hour of sleep anymore, and it stopped complaining. It became accustomed to getting up at that hour. I also believe for supernatural rest when I have a short night. It works!

The decision to make time for God every morning has been one of the most important decisions of my life. It made such a difference in my spiritual growth. I'm not the same person I was then. People are always talking about how timid and restrained I used to be. I really was, too, but I got over it!

Become Addicted to Jesus

By implementing the changes God instructed me to make, I created a lifestyle of living contact with God. I became addicted to spending time with Him. Do you know what the word *addicted* means? It means "to devote, to deliver over, to apply habitually."

You can create good habits in God the same way you can create poor habits. If you'll habitually apply yourself to making contact with Him daily through prayer and The WORD, it will become a way of life to you. You won't even have to think about doing it. It will just come naturally to you.

That's what happened to me. I have developed such a habit of making time with God my first priority that I don't have to get up every day and think, *Well, should I read The WORD and pray this morning?* I just do it automatically. It's a way of life for me to spend the first part of my day in prayer now. Even when Ken and I are traveling, even when I have to get up at 4 o'clock in the morning to do it—I do it.

You might think that's extreme. You might think I'm the only one around who is that committed to spending time with The LORD every day, but I'm not. I'm one of many.

Certainly, such faithfulness requires time and effort. It's not easy. But if believers fully understood THE BLESSING it brings, they too would be willing to do whatever was necessary in order to make their time with God their first priority every day.

There are great rewards for that kind of faithfulness! The Bible says, "The eyes of The LORD run to and fro throughout the whole earth, to show himself strong in the behalf of them whose heart is perfect toward him" (2 Chronicles 16:9). The word translated *perfect* there doesn't mean without a flaw. It simply means "faithful, loyal, dedicated and devoted."

God will pass over a million people to find that one who is loyal to Him. He scans the earth looking for people who will put Him first and let Him be God in their lives.

But God can't bless us as He wants to if we won't let Him be God in our lives. He can't pour out His provision on us if we keep clogging up our heavenly supply line by putting other things before Him. If He is to show Himself strong on our behalf, our hearts will have to be turned wholly toward Him.

The bottom line is this: The eternal, all-powerful Creator of heaven and earth, the Almighty God, is ready right now to meet with you in prayer. He's made your prayers His priority. The question is, have you?

Daily Reflection

What is prayer?

_____

_____

What role does prayer play in your fellowship with other believers?

_____

_____

How do you know you can come "boldly unto the throne of grace"?

_____

_____

How can a habit become an addiction?

_____

_____

_____

_____

_____

What steps will you take to make prayer a priority in your life?

_____

_____

_____

_____

_____

_____

_____

_____

_____

Today's
Prayer of Faith

Heavenly Father, I commit to spending time with You daily in prayer, fellowshiping with You and submitting to Your will in every area of my life. Thank You for helping me to be faithful, loyal, dedicated and devoted!

Real-Life Testimonies
to Help Build Your Faith

Living Prayer

I prayed for a woman at a small prayer meeting I help lead, and she was completely healed of three lumps in her breast and swollen lymph nodes under her arm that the mammography clinic thought might be cancer. She went to her doctor to get tested two days later and all was completely gone! Thank you for discipling me for these years and helping my faith build to believe God for the miraculous. God bless you.

Chelsea C.
Washington

Chapter Two
Hearing His Voice and Acting on It

Today, you'll discover:

How people who pray participate in what God is doing in the earth

What we can learn from Simeon and Anna

How the Holy Spirit communicates with us

The key to every door in God's kingdom.

The Place of Prayer
by Kenneth Copeland

There is a particular phrase I've heard spoken countless times over the years, and I like it less every time I hear it. No doubt, you've heard it too.

It comes most frequently on the heels of some tragedy. It's said—usually in drawn-out, religious-sounding tones—when circumstances seem to fall short of what God has promised us in His WORD.

The phrase is "Well, Brother, you have to remember...God is sovereign."

As spiritual as that phrase might sound, it really bothers me. It's not that I don't believe God is sovereign. Certainly He is. According to *Webster's New World College Dictionary, Fourth Edition, sovereign* means "above or superior to all others; supreme in power, rank or authority." Without question, God is all those things.

But all too often, when people refer to the sovereignty of God, what they're actually saying is, "You never know what God will do. After all, He's all-powerful and totally independent, so He does whatever He wants, whenever He wants."

The problem with that view of sovereignty is it releases us of all responsibility. After all, if God is sovereign, He will do what He wants anyway, so we might as well go watch TV and forget about it, right?

Wrong. After more than 40 years of studying The WORD and preaching the gospel, I've come to realize that God does very few things—if any—in this earth without man's cooperation. Even though it belongs to God—it is His creation and He owns it. Psalm 8:6 tells us God has made man "to have dominion over the works of [God's] hands."

God Himself put mankind in charge. He doesn't intervene in the affairs of earth whenever He wants to. He respects the dominion and authority He has given us. So, until man's lease on this planet expires, God restricts His power on the earth, taking action only when He is asked to do so.

Since the people who pray often do their praying in secret, it may appear at times that God simply acts on His own. But regardless of appearances, the Bible teaches from cover to cover that God's connection with man is a prayer and faith connection. When you see Him act in a mighty way, you can be sure there was someone, somewhere praying and interceding to bring Him on the scene.

More Than Spectators

Now more than ever before, it is vital for every Christian to understand that. We are in the last of the last days. We are on the edge of the greatest outpouring of God's glory this earth has ever seen. Amazing, supernatural things are beginning to happen just as the Bible said they would.

Yet many believers are just sitting back, watching these events like spiritual spectators. They seem to think God will sovereignly turn over some great heavenly glory bucket and spill signs and wonders over the earth. But it won't happen that way.

How will it happen? Acts 2:17-19 shows us:

And it shall come to pass in the last days, saith God, I will pour out of my Spirit upon all flesh: and your sons and your daughters shall prophesy, and your young men shall see visions, and your old men shall dream dreams: And on my servants and on my handmaidens I will pour out in those days of my Spirit; and they shall prophesy: And I will show wonders in heaven above, and signs in the earth beneath.

If you'll read the last part of that passage again, taking out the punctuation that was put in by the translators, you'll see a divine connection most people miss. You'll see that God is saying when His servants and handmaidens prophesy, speaking out His divine will and purpose in intercession and faith, He responds to their speaking by working signs and wonders and miracles.

That means if this last outpouring of glory is to come in its fullness, each of God's servants and handmaidens must be in his or her place. What place?

The place of prayer!

Some people would say, "Well, Brother Copeland, we're talking about end-time events here, and I believe God will simply bring them about on His own. He doesn't need any help from us. After all, those things are too important to entrust to mere men."

That's what I used to think, too. But God set me straight some years ago. At the time, I had been studying the authority of man and had seen over and over in His WORD how the prayers of God's people precede God's actions on the earth. Yet I still hung on to the idea that God still did His most important works independently of man.

One day as I was praying about it, I said, "Lord, You brought Jesus into the earth sovereignly, didn't You?"

No, I didn't, He answered.

"You mean there were people who interceded for the birth of Jesus?" I asked.

Yes.

Then He told me the names of two of them—Simeon and Anna.

50 Years of Prayer

You can find the scriptural account of these two intercessors in Luke 2. There, the Bible tells us that when Jesus was 8 days old, His parents took Him to the temple to be dedicated to The LORD and circumcised into the Abrahamic covenant.

This ceremony was very sacred to the Jewish people, yet right in the middle of it, a man named Simeon walked in and took the baby Jesus in his arms. Nobody said anything to him. Nobody tried to stop him. So it's obvious he was well-known in the temple as a very spiritual man.

How did Simeon know to go to the temple at that particular time? Was it because someone came and told him that Jesus was being dedicated? No, the Bible tells us "he came by the Spirit" (verse 27). He was led there by God.

What's more, even though Mary herself didn't yet understand who this child of hers truly was, Simeon did, and he prophesied, saying: "Lord, now lettest thou thy servant depart in peace, according to thy word: For mine eyes have seen thy salvation, which thou hast prepared before the face of all people; a light to lighten the Gentiles, and the glory of thy people Israel" (verses 29-32).

Simeon knew who Jesus was because he had interceded, asking God to send the Redeemer. He had prayed so fervently and so long that God had promised him "that he should not see death, before he had seen The LORD's Christ" (verse 26).

It is amazing enough that Simeon recognized Jesus as the Savior of Israel, but his words reveal he knew even more than that. Read again what Simeon said, and you'll see that he knew Jesus was bringing salvation to the Gentiles—a fact the rest of the Church didn't find out until Peter went to Cornelius' house, 10 years after the day of Pentecost!

Why was Simeon so wise? He was an intercessor. Intercessors know things other people don't know. God tells them divine secrets and mysteries. He gives them inside information.

When Simeon finished prophesying over Jesus that day, in walked a little woman named Anna who had been a widow 84 years (verses 36-37, *The Amplified Bible*). Unlike Simeon, this woman didn't have to be led to the temple by the Holy Spirit—she was already there. In fact, the Bible tells us she "departed not from the temple, but served God with fastings and prayers night and day" (verse 37).

She hadn't just been there for a week or two, either. She had been residing there ever since her husband died. She had been praying in the temple for over 80 years.

That's what I call staying with the program!

Luke 2:38 says that Anna "coming in that instant gave thanks likewise unto The LORD, and spake of him to all them that looked for redemption in Jerusalem." No one had to tell her who Jesus was. She knew the moment she saw Him because, like Simeon, she had been praying for God to send Him for many years.

Just think—even though God is the Almighty, Supreme Creator of this universe, He did not send Jesus into the earth independently. He did it in cooperation with men. He did it in response to the faith-filled words and prayers of His people.

Matthew 18:19 says, "If two of you shall agree on earth as touching any thing that they shall ask, it shall be done for them of my Father which is in heaven." Whether Simeon and Anna knew it or not, they were praying in agreement. They had both interceded, asking God to send His Redeemer—and God answered.

Get With the Program!

What does that mean to us today? It means if we want to see the fullness of this final outpouring of glory, we must get with the program as Anna did. We must get on our knees and start praying for it. We must start speaking out God's WORD and His will for this last hour in prophecy and intercession so He can do signs and wonders.

You see, there are certain things that will never happen on the earth unless someone speaks them. If you'll read through the Bible, you'll discover there are certain events that had to be foretold by the prophets before God would bring them to pass.

I'm not saying Jesus won't come back if you don't pray. Jesus is coming for His people—and He is coming soon. This world has had all the sin it will stand, and it's about to come apart. The whole creation is groaning under the stress of it. God will close out this age just as He said He would in His WORD—no matter what you and I do. He'll find a Simeon and an Anna somewhere to get the job done.

But if all the believers will pray, instead of just a few, He'll increase the outpouring of glory that will accompany His return. If we'll cry out to God in one accord as the early Church did in Acts 4, this earth will be shaken by the power of God.

God cannot sit still when He hears the cries of His people!

God hasn't changed. He is doing the same thing in our day that He did in Acts. But this time, He is moving even more powerfully and gloriously than He did then.

Does your heart hunger to experience that end-time outpouring? Do you want to see firsthand the supernatural signs and wonders He will perform in these last days? Then get in the place of prayer! Become an intercessor, yielding to the Spirit of God in prayer and speaking out His will.

Today's Connection Points

⊙ **Worship CD: "When I Speak Your Name" (Track 2)**

Speak the mighty Name of Jesus today and see mountains move as He answers your prayer.

⊙ **DVD: "Praying In the Spirit" (Chapter 2)**

The Holy Spirit helps you pray God's will. Kenneth shares how this is the key to releasing His power in your life.

Faith in Action

✋ ***Realize that you play a role in what God is doing!***
Commit to recognizing His promptings and responding in prayer today.

Notes:

_____

_____

_____

_____

_____

_____

_____

_____

_____

_____

_____

_____

_____

_____

_____

_____

_____

_____

_____

_____

Was That Me, Lord, or You?
by Gloria Copeland

Do you ever have trouble hearing from God? Do you ever find yourself caught in confusing circumstances needing guidance, and yet even after praying and reading The WORD, you're still not sure what God wants you to do?

I've had that experience. For years that was a weak area in my life with God. I knew His written WORD and I loved it. Acting on it had changed my life.

But I was uncertain when I had to make decisions about things The WORD didn't specifically address. Things like whether to move to one city or another, for example, or whether to take this opportunity or that one.

When I faced that kind of decision, I'd pray about it. I usually made the right decisions because I wouldn't make any major changes until I had peace in my heart. I learned from *The Amplified Bible* to let peace be the umpire (Colossians 3:15). But even so, there was uncertainty. "Was that me, Lord, or was that You?"

I did have one thing going for me though, even then. I had a deep willingness to obey God. Right from the beginning I saw in The WORD that God couldn't bless disobedient people. So I didn't have a problem with disobedience holding me back. I'd been eager to obey God ever since I got into His WORD.

The good news is that when we spend time daily praying in the spirit, it becomes easier for us to hear the direction of the Holy Spirit as He reveals His will to our spirits.

Recognize the Promptings

"So now we serve not under [obedience to] the old code of written regulations, but [under obedience to the promptings] of the Spirit in newness [of life]" (Romans 7:6, *The Amplified Bible*). We are no longer bound to obey written regulations, but we are to serve by obeying the promptings of our reborn spirits, which are controlled by the Holy Spirit. The Holy Spirit communicates with our spirits. He dwells in our spirits.

I believe this is an area of confusion when we are learning to walk in the spirit. As The LORD was clarifying this to me, He made me realize that most of the time I would hear my own spirit speaking to my soul, which is my mind, will and emotions. The audible voice of The LORD is rare in most of our lives. Almost every leading we will receive in everyday life will be a prompting, an impression, a thought, an inward witness, a leading or an unction from our spirits.

The reason it sounds like us is because it is ourselves that we hear. The Holy Spirit communicates with our spirits, and our spirits prompt, or enlighten, our minds.

You see, when you were born again, God sent His Holy Spirit to live in you and be your teacher and trainer to help you live a life that is pleasing to God. That's His job.

That's why, as believers, we don't have to depend on our own limited reasoning. We can live guided by the Spirit who knows all things. In fact, if we'll listen to Him on a daily basis, He'll steer us clear of hidden dangers and maneuver us safely through even the most complicated situations.

How do you let Him steer you? You'll find the answer to that question in Hebrews 3:15. It says, "Wherefore, as the Holy Ghost says, Today if you will hear His voice, *harden not your hearts."* In other words, don't resist the promptings of the Spirit.

When you sense Him directing you to do something and you decide, consciously or unconsciously, "No, I don't want to do that, I think I'll go another way," you've just hardened your heart.

Most of the time, that's how we miss the will of God. We're not trying to be rebellious. It's just that in one situation after another we didn't follow that leading in our spirits. Our minds, or reasoning, told us the 27 reasons why we shouldn't. So we didn't.

A few years ago I specifically asked God to teach me how to walk in the spirit. As I listened for His leading, I could sense Him prompting me to spend more time in prayer. Until then, I'd spent most of my time in The WORD. But God began to deal with me about spending more time in prayer, especially praying in the spirit.

So I began to set aside an hour a day just for that. It was very inconvenient, I can tell you. I had to rearrange plans and circumstances. I had to switch around my whole routine.

But before that year was out, my life had changed dramatically. Yet the only thing I'd done differently was spend an hour a day praying in the spirit.

An hour may not sound like a very long time, and it isn't. But I'll tell you what, I did it EVERY DAY. And that's the key. Once, while I was studying The WORD, God said to me, *In consistency lies the power.*

It's being consistent in the things of God that causes us to walk in victory. Going after God in spurts won't do it.

Do you know how to fulfill the will of God for your life? One day at a time. If you'll begin to spend time with Him daily and pray in the spirit, you'll look back next year at this time and realize that your spiritual life and ability to hear from God has increased.

Make a Commitment

Start today by making a commitment to do just the simple things He tells you to do. Start seeking His face, listening for His promptings and responding in obedience instead of hardening your heart.

Don't be afraid He's going to ask you to part the Red Sea the first day. He won't. He starts where you are. He's the master Teacher. He knows how to deal with you perfectly. And He will bring you into His perfect will if you'll just obey Him one step at a time, one day at a time.

I've learned though, that if you're going to do this you'll have to become like a little child. You have to be simple enough to trust Him and do whatever He tells you to do.

I remember, at first, when The LORD would tell me to do something, I wouldn't want to because I'd think, *If that's not You, Lord, I'm going to look really dumb.*

Did you know that's exactly what keeps us from walking in the spirit? Thinking about our "image"—caring more about how we look to people than about how we look to God.

I wrestled and wrestled with those kinds of concerns until finally one day I decided, *OK, when I sense God's prompting in my spirit, I'm going to do it. So what if I make a mistake sometime and wind up looking dumb? That'll be good for me. It'll keep me humble.*

Once I made that decision, obeying the voice of God became much simpler. And it was amazing how much easier it was to act on what I'd heard.

Jesus said in Matthew 18:4, "Whosoever therefore shall humble himself as this little child, the same is greatest in the kingdom of heaven." And that's what I finally did. I decided I'd rather look ridiculous than risk being disobedient.

When you come to that point, you're on the verge of an enormous break-through in your life with God because as you follow His promptings, they grow clearer in your spirit.

I've discovered that the key to every door in God's kingdom is obedience. It's not what you say you're *going* to do, it's what you actually do that counts with God. When you're ready to obey the Spirit, you're also ready to hear Him.

If that kind of adventure is what you want, you can say to God just what I said back in 1983: "Lord, show me how to walk in Your Spirit and I'll do it. Teach me how to hear Your voice. I don't care what I look like. You teach me and I'll do it." (Of course, when you obey, *you* look good!)

Pray that now and mean it, and you'll be opening the door to the greatest adventure of your life.

Daily Reflection

How do people who pray participate in what God is doing in the earth?

_____

_____

_____

What can we learn from Simeon and Anna?

_____

_____

_____

How does the Holy Spirit communicate with us?

_____

_____

_____

What's the key to every door in God's kingdom?

_____

_____

_____

Notes:

_____

_____

_____

_____

_____

_____

_____

_____

_____

_____

_____

_____

_____

_____

_____

Today's Prayer of Faith

Father, I want to be Your vessel for working in the earth. Help me to always hear Your voice, and I will obey it. Show me how to walk in Your Spirit. In Jesus' Name. Amen.

Real-Life Testimonies
to Help Build Your Faith

Prosperity Close to Home

Hallelujah! Praise to Jesus! This fall I called your prayer line for intercessory prayer to manifest a new job. God gave me a wonderful position with a prosperous, national corporation, only five minutes from my home. Thank you so much for caring!

Catherine E.
Maine

Chapter Three
Praying God's Will

Today, you'll discover:

Where you can always find God's will

What "don't pray your problem" means

Why it's important to pray in the spirit

How your life will change when you pray in tongues consistently.

Why It's Important to Pray God's Will:
Harvest! by Kenneth Copeland

I f there ever was a time we needed to pray, it is now.

It's a time for prayer because of the darkness the world is going through. Satan is killing people with disease, drugs, depression and every other weapon he can get in his hands.

It's time to pray because this generation of believers is in a very, very special time in history. We are at the end of an age. The 6,000 years of man's lease (and Satan's lordship) on the earth are coming to a close. The 1,000 years of Jesus' millennial reign are immediately ahead.

But before Jesus comes, God will fulfill every promise He has made during the 6,000 years of man's history on earth. The Body of the Anointed One is about to have its hands full of harvest.

The key to seeing the kind of results God wants His last-days generation to walk in is not just shooting some scatter-shot type of prayer, and hoping something might happen. James wrote, "Ye have not, because ye ask not. Ye ask, and receive not, because ye ask amiss, that ye may consume it upon your lusts" (James 4:2-3). Success comes when we pray accurately according to the will of God.

Praying the Will of God

So many believers wring their hands and worry about whether or not they're praying according to God's will. As I mentioned in the last session, many of them have been taught a wrong view of God's sovereignty. They think that His ways are past finding out, and it is more spiritual to pray, "God, whatever Your will is in this situation, You just go ahead and do it."

Just think what kind of confusion that causes. Whatever results from that kind of praying is credited to God—good or bad! To really honor God's sovereignty, we must pray what He has already declared to be His will.

Praying the will of God is the only kind of praying that can consistently, confidently be expected to bring results. We weren't created to waste time standing around looking puzzled, especially in these days. We need to grab our Bibles and find out what the will of God is. God's WORD *is* His will. He has made some very specific promises in it. And it's His will to fulfill every one of them.

Think about what you did when you prayed for salvation. You didn't pray, "God, I'm sick and tired of this life under Satan's control, and I want You to be my Lord and Savior. But I don't want to tell You what to do. Whatever Your will is—to set me free or to keep me in this miserable condition, to send me to heaven or to send me to hell—You just do it."

No. You prayed for God to save you just like His WORD said He would. You prayed accurately according to His WORD that He is "not willing that any should perish" (2 Peter 3:9). You prayed expecting results according to the promise: "If thou shalt confess with thy mouth The LORD Jesus, and shalt believe in thine heart that God hath raised him from the dead, thou shalt be saved" (Romans 10:9).

Maybe you wondered at first, *Did God hear me?*, then later discovered that 1 John 5:14-15 says, "If we ask any thing according to his will, he heareth us: And if we know that he hear us; whatsoever we ask, we know that we have the petitions that we desired of him."

Find Out What The WORD Says

These same principles work in any area of prayer. Do you need healing in your body? Don't pray what the doctor says or what your religious tradition has told you. Pray "by His stripes [I am] healed" (1 Peter 2:24). Do you have financial needs? Don't pray your problem. Pray what God has said He will do: "My God shall supply all [my] need according to His riches in glory by Christ Jesus" (Philippians 4:19).

God wants His will to be done on earth as it is in heaven. Find the promise that applies to your situation and pray the answer instead of the problem. Don't just pray what you *remember* The WORD of God says. Read it! Even if you've read that promise a hundred times, read it again. Feed on what it says again and again. One day, you'll read a familiar verse and suddenly God will give you the greatest revelation you've ever had in your life. And it will be exactly what you need to know to pray effectively about your current situation.

First John 5:14-15 says, "This is the confidence that we have in him, that, if we ask any thing according to his will, he heareth us: And if we know that he hear us, whatsoever we ask, we know that we have the petitions that we desired of him."

When you pray God's WORD, knowing His will in advance, you are no longer praying just *hoping* to get results. You're not rattling off a bunch of religious-sounding words. You're praying *expecting* to get results. You're praying accurately because you are praying the very words God has given as His will to be done on earth.

So, before you pray, make the decision to get results, then pray The WORD, expecting God to move. That's the way we bring demonstrations of God's glory on earth while people are being increasingly tempted and terrorized by Satan's deception. That's the way we position ourselves to receive harvest that will come so quickly that the sower overtakes the reaper.

Jesus is the Alpha and Omega—the Beginning and the End—the First and Last. So let's start with His WORD and finish with His WORD. Give Jesus the first word in everything you do, and watch Him bring in a harvest like no previous generation has ever seen!

Today's Connection Points

⊙ **Worship CD: "Hope for the Future" (Track 3)**

God has *great* hope for your future! As you enter into worship today, be confident He is with you and answers your every prayer.

⊙ **DVD: "Believe What You Pray" (Chapter 3)**

Kenneth teaches how to pray God's WORD every time and believe it will come to pass.

Faith in Action

 *Search God's WORD for specific promises you can stand on for a situation you're facing.*
Then, pray those promises.

Notes:

_____

_____

_____

_____

_____

_____

_____

_____

_____

_____

_____

_____

_____

_____

_____

_____

Praying the Perfect Will of God

by Gloria Copeland

Near the end of 1982 I heard a prophecy that changed my life. The LORD gave me direction and instruction. This word from The LORD impressed on me that if I would just give a tithe of my time, an hour or two a day to The LORD, all would be well, my life would be changed and empowered. At the time, I especially thought about my family. I needed things well in my family.

One result of this exhortation by God's Spirit is that God led me to pray in the spirit an hour each day. At that time, even five minutes seemed long to me. I just did not spend much time in prayer. I concentrated on God's written WORD. I would go to Him, show Him His WORD, believe it, act on it and it would come to pass in my life. But I had never spent much time in prayer. This word from God changed my life.

It has been more than 20 years since I decided to spend an hour or two with God every day. It has been of major importance to my spiritual growth and the well-being of my present life. I sincerely believe that all my needs are met abundantly today because I obeyed this direction. My children are serving The LORD. My grandchildren are well and happy. My children have blessed and happy marriages, and they are prospering. We are *all* well.

Ken and I are still happy and in love with each other after nearly 50 years. I believe we have run the race God set before us and obeyed His will for our lives up to the present day. Yes, I am still spending at least an hour in prayer every morning. I like for all to be well!

But this prophecy wasn't just to me. It was to the Church. Spending time with God every day for an hour or two in His presence in prayer, in The WORD, praising Him, going to church services—will change your life as well.

The important thing is to do what God tells *you* to do and to be consistent in the things of God. Spending time in eternal things is not like spending time in the affairs of this world. Your prayers are eternal, and eternal things never end. They have everlasting reward.

Praying in the Spirit

Likewise the Spirit also helpeth our infirmities: for we know not what we should pray for as we ought: but the Spirit itself maketh intercession for us with groanings which cannot be uttered. And he that searcheth the hearts knoweth what is the mind of the Spirit, because he maketh intercession for the saints according to the will of God (Romans 8:26-27).

When I began to pray an hour each day, I prayed mostly in the spirit—in other tongues. Often we don't know how to pray as we ought. But the Spirit of God knows. The Spirit of God is in you to pray through you—to give you utterance in the perfect will of God. That is what praying in other tongues is all about. He prays God's answer through you. The WORD says, "He that speaketh in an unknown tongue speaketh not unto men, but unto God…" (1 Corinthians 14:2).

You may ask, "But can't I pray in my own language?"

Yes, but not to the degree you need to be praying. You can only pray with your own understanding according to the knowledge you have. Many times you will not know enough in the natural to accurately pray for the answer, but the Holy Spirit inside you will provide God's solution when you pray in the spirit. The Holy Spirit prays God's higher way into the situation—His perfect will.

In 1 Corinthians 14:15, the Apostle Paul said we should pray both ways: "What is it then? I will pray with the spirit, and I will pray with the understanding also: I will sing with the spirit, and I will sing with the understanding also."

The Holy Spirit is in us to bring to pass the will of God in our lives. Bringing to pass God's will is the pre-eminent responsibility of the Church in the earth. But because the Church is made up of individual people, this responsibility starts with you and me. Each person in the Church being obedient to the Spirit of God, will cause God's will to be done in the earth.

Be Filled

If you don't yet speak in tongues, you don't have to beg God to give you this empowering of His Spirit. All any born-again believer has to do is ask. If you will ask, The WORD of God promises you shall receive:

> And I say unto you, Ask, and it shall be given you; seek, and ye shall find; knock, and it shall be opened unto you. For every one that asketh receiveth; and he that seeketh findeth; and to him that knocketh it shall be opened. If a son shall ask bread of any of you that is a father, will he give him a stone? or if he ask a fish, will he for a fish give him a serpent? Or if he shall ask an egg, will he offer him a scorpion? If ye then, being evil, know how to give good gifts unto your children: *how much more* shall your heavenly Father give the Holy Spirit to them that ask him? (Luke 11:9-13).

Jesus is speaking about a son asking something of his father. You are a son of God—His child—and He is your Father. If you go to God and ask for the Holy Spirit, you won't get a devil. Don't be worried about getting the wrong thing.

God is poised and ready to baptize you in His Holy Spirit when you ask Him.

Receiving the Holy Spirit requires that you humble yourself before God. Stand before Him, open and ready to receive the Holy Spirit by faith.

When you are baptized in the Holy Spirit, an extraordinary thing happens: You are able to speak in another language you did not learn. "And they were all filled with the Holy Ghost, and began to speak with other tongues, as the Spirit gave them utterance" (Acts 2:4). The Holy Spirit gives you the utterance, or the words to say, but *you* must do the speaking. Nowhere in the New Testament does it say that the Holy Spirit does the speaking. God will not force you to speak in tongues.

When you pray in tongues, you are praying "in the spirit." Just as your native language is the voice of your mind, praying in tongues is the voice of your spirit. It is your spirit speaking mysteries to God (1 Corinthians 14:2). The Apostle Paul said, "If I pray in an unknown tongue, my spirit prayeth, but my understanding is unfruitful" (1 Corinthians 14:14). Pray now to receive the Holy Spirit:

My heavenly Father, I am a believer. I am Your child and You are my Father. Jesus is my Lord. I believe with all my heart that Your WORD is true.

Your WORD says that if I will ask I will receive the Holy Spirit, so in the Name of Jesus Christ, my LORD, I am asking You to fill me to overflowing with Your precious Holy Spirit.

Jesus, baptize me in the Holy Spirit. Because of Your WORD, I believe I now receive and I thank You for it. I believe the Holy Spirit is within me and by faith I accept it.

Now, Holy Spirit, rise up within me as I praise my God. I fully expect to speak with other tongues as You give me the utterance.

Now, begin to thank and praise God for baptizing you in the Holy Spirit. As you do, there will rise up within your spirit certain words and syllables that are unknown to you, so by faith, speak them. Don't speak anymore in your own language. You can't speak two languages at the same time. Just begin to speak the syllables that are on your lips. You are like a baby and you will begin by speaking baby-sounding words. (Remember, you have to use your own voice. God will not force you to speak.)

From this moment on, you are a Holy Spirit-baptized believer!

What If We All Prayed in the Spirit?

When The LORD led me to pray an hour each day, it changed my life. Now I pray in English as much as in the spirit—just whatever direction I receive.

If you prayed in the spirit one hour a day, by the end of the year you would have prayed 365 hours of the perfect will of God. Just 15 minutes a day would be 91 hours. Don't you think that would affect everything in your life for good? It certainly did mine. I wouldn't consider not spending time in prayer every morning.

I want you to realize that God will deal with you right where you are today. He might tell you to pray five minutes each day. He may ask you to start there and then increase. Five minutes is important when you are praying the perfect will of God. It is God praying through you. He gives the utterance, you give Him your authority and your voice. Your intellect will not get in the way because you are not praying out of your head, but out of your spirit.

We must come to a place where we keep God's WORD, obey His guidance and simply do what we are told—a body of people that God can depend on to do His will in the earth.

What God said exactly was, *Don't take up all your time with natural things...but see to it that you give heed unto your spirit and give your spirit opportunity to feed upon My WORD...and give your spirit opportunity to commune with the Father above and build yourself up on your most holy faith...just an hour or two out of 24, just pay a tithe of your time unto Me, saith The LORD, and all will be well.*

Daily Reflection

Where can you always find God's will?

_____

_____

What does "don't pray your problem" mean?

_____

_____

Why is it important to pray in the spirit?

_____

_____

How would your life change if you prayed in tongues consistently?

_____

_____

_____

_____

Today's Prayer of Faith

Father, more than anything, I want to follow Your will for my life. Today, I commit to pray in the spirit and to pray with my understanding. As I do, may Your will be done in every area of my life! In Jesus' Name. Amen.

Real-Life Testimonies
To Help Build Your Faith

God's Will for Promotion

In May, I had a group of believing ladies pray for God's perfect will for jobs for my husband and me. I was up for a promotion but wanted only God's will for it. My husband was discontent at his current job and they were not paying him well. In August, I got the word that I did not get the promotion but I was so thrilled. My current job is nine hours per week as a college teacher. Because it is part time, I have time to pick up my daughter after school, minister to people, attend a women's Bible study and pray longer on certain days.

In September, my husband left his other job and after a week of vacation, which had been previously planned, he found out about another job that was part time. He took it. During that week, the full-time employee of the company left. My husband had so impressed his boss that he was moved to full time the next week! The boss really likes him. He is so happy in this job. It starts later in the day so he is able to take our daughter to school.

God takes care of every detail. This week, the boss let him hire a helper, and my husband was able to get a Christian friend into this work. THE BLESSING keeps working and working wherever we go!

Rachelle M.
Massachusetts

Chapter Four
Praying With Confidence

Today, you'll discover:

Why it's important to speak only words that agree with what you desire

How you can stop doubt

What weakness everyone faces

Some additional benefits of praying in tongues.

Praying for Results
by Kenneth Copeland

When you begin your prayer based on God's WORD, you are starting with the answer. The WORD contains the answer to every problem that could confront you.

The next step in praying effectively is found in Mark 11:24. Jesus said, "What things soever ye desire, when ye pray, believe that ye receive them, and ye shall have them." This places a qualification on your prayer. You must believe you receive when you pray. Don't wait until the manifestation comes to believe you receive.

This will seem very difficult at first. But as you get to know God personally, you will become convinced His WORD is true. The problem area will diminish. Make a quality decision to believe God's WORD. Numbers 23:19 says, "God is not a man, that he should lie; neither the son of man, that he should repent: hath he said, and shall he not do it? or hath he spoken, and shall he not make it good?" You can trust His integrity. When you pray, all you have to do is apply your faith.

Where does faith come from? How do you get it? Romans 10:17 says faith comes by hearing, and hearing by The WORD of God. Every believer is dealt the measure of faith (Romans 12:3). He must develop that faith by spending time in The WORD of God. The application of your faith, in any given situation, is directly related to your knowledge of God. You could not have faith to be saved before you knew it was God's will to save you. If you feel you need more faith, realize that you already have it. What you need is a more personal knowledge of God, through time in His WORD.

Once you have prayed in faith, hold fast to your confession. God is aware of your situation. His power went to work the instant you prayed in faith. You can now rest assured that what you prayed will come to pass. Maintain your faith by keeping your confession—what you say—in line with The WORD.

Speak only words that agree with what you desire. Jesus is seated at the right hand of the Father. As your High Priest, He is seeing to it that the whole system works the way God said it would (Hebrews 4:9-14)!

The importance of speaking right words cannot be measured. Faith is released with the mouth. Words are the vehicles. God spoke faith-filled words when He created the universe. Hebrews 11:3 says, "Through faith we understand that the worlds were framed by The WORD of God...." God spoke and the Spirit of God used the faith in those words to create the worlds.

Words carry power. The very forces of life and death are powered by the tongue (Proverbs 18:21). Ask the Holy Spirit to reveal to you the importance of speaking right words.

Put It Into Action

When faith words are spoken, they must be backed by corresponding actions. James 2:17, *The Amplified Bible,* says, "So also faith, if it does not have works (deeds and actions of obedience to back it up), by itself is destitute of power (inoperative, dead)." God's WORD instructs us to be doers of what it says and not hearers only. In applying faith, two elements are involved: words and actions. Real Bible faith demands action.

You have to act by faith, not according to your feelings or reasonings. Faith is based on eternal truth and is more dependable than the evidence of your physical senses. According to 2 Corinthians 4:18, we are not to look at things which are seen, but at things which are not seen. The things which are visible are *temporal,* or changeable. The things which are invisible are eternal—they never change. Don't focus your attention on what you perceive through your five physical senses. Keep your heart fixed on The WORD of God. Then what you see will come in line with The WORD.

To believe God's WORD, rather than physical circumstances, is to talk and act the answer instead of the problem. Acting on The WORD puts faith in motion. You cannot expect results from your prayer without the operation of faith.

When you apply your faith accurately, according to God's WORD, you will get results. You will experience Hebrews 4:16 for yourself. "Let us therefore come boldly unto the throne of grace, that we may obtain mercy, and find grace to help in time of need." It does not say, "Come and hope to get." It says, "Come and obtain"!

A very misunderstood concept throughout the religious world, is that it is extremely difficult to get God to answer prayer at all—much less answer all prayer. That is a lie of Satan and absolutely contrary to The WORD of God. When you believe God's WORD in your heart, and pray in line with His WORD, you have every right to expect your prayer to bring results. Jesus said, "Verily I say unto you, If ye have faith, and doubt not, ye shall not only do this which is done to the fig tree, but also if ye shall say unto this mountain, Be thou removed, and be thou cast into the sea; it shall be done. And all things, whatsoever ye shall ask in prayer, believing, ye shall receive" (Matthew 21:21-22).

If God will answer the prayer of a sinner to be saved, He will certainly answer the prayers of born-again believers who come to Him in faith concerning their lives.

Refusing Doubt

Satan uses doubt with great skill and cunning to cause you to fail. He knows the importance of getting you to waver. He constantly tries to throw doubt and unbelief into your consciousness. If you begin to wonder whether you have the answer, Satan will purpose to secure a foothold in your mind. By gradually increasing his influence, he knows your faith will become ineffective and cause you to be defeated.

In praying effectively, a vital part of your success is knowing how to refuse doubt, fear and unbelief. If you are concentrating on your circumstances instead of The WORD, you are building an inner image of the problem and not the solution. What you see on the inside will determine your attitude. If all you envision is your negative circumstances, you will doubt God's WORD. Satan will then be able to take advantage of you to thwart your faith process.

Doubt operates in the mental realm. God's WORD operates in the spiritual realm. Our responsibility is to use the spiritual weapons at our disposal. Second Corinthians 10:3-5 says, "For though we walk in the flesh, we do not war after the flesh: (For the weapons of our warfare are not carnal, but mighty through God to the pulling down of strong holds;) casting down imaginations, and every high thing that exalteth itself against the knowledge of God, and bringing into captivity every thought to the obedience of Christ." In Matthew 14, when Peter walked on the water with Jesus, his battle was not with natural forces. The combat was spiritual. Natural law was subject to the power inherent in Jesus' word, "Come." By stepping out of the boat, Peter acted on the authority in that word.

We can walk in the supernatural in spite of life's storms raging against us. Our spiritual weapons are mighty!

Do not allow doubt or fear to enter your consciousness. Maintain control of your mind. Be ready to refuse any thought or imagination contrary to your prayer. When doubt comes, refuse to give it any place. Be selective about the thoughts you entertain. Do not build inner images of defeat! You can control your thought life according to Philippians 4:6-9. Learn to think on things that are true, honest, just, pure, lovely and of good report.

Satan uses doubt and fear to bluff you into accepting defeat. But you can overcome him by the power of God and faith in His WORD.

Today's
Connection Points

⊙ **Worship CD: "Your Name" (Track 4)**

Glorify the Name of The LORD today as you pray with unshakable confidence.

⊙ **DVD: "Stop Doubt" (Chapter 4)**

Stop doubt and unbelief. Kenneth shares how to keep from speaking words that are contrary to The WORD of God.

Faith
in Action

✋ *Approach The LORD in confidence today, refusing to doubt.*

Keep yourself strong by praying in tongues.

Notes:

_____

_____

_____

_____

_____

_____

_____

_____

_____

_____

_____

_____

_____

_____

_____

_____

_____

_____

_____

_____

_____

The Power of Praying in Tongues

by Gloria Copeland

Since we started talking about this last session, I want to take a moment to mention a few more benefits of praying in tongues. Because, let's face it: You have a weakness. It doesn't matter who you are...or how often you work out at the local gym. If you're a born-again child of God living on planet Earth, you have a weakness. It's a weakness that can knock your legs out from under you just when you think you're standing strong. It can cause you to act like a sinner on the outside, when on the inside you're a saint.

What is that weakness? Your flesh.

That's right. That flesh-and-blood body you live in hasn't been reborn as your spirit has. If it controls your life, it will take you from one failure to another. And believe me, if you don't do something to stop it, it will take control.

What you have to do is build up your spirit—strengthen it to the point where it can actually dominate, or rule over, your flesh. If that sounds hard, don't worry. It's not. In fact, God has made it so easy that anyone can do it. Jude 20 will show you how. It says: "But you, beloved, build yourselves up [founded] on your most holy faith—make progress, rise like an edifice higher and higher—praying in the Holy Spirit" *(The Amplified Bible)*.

Most believers don't realize it, but praying in the spirit, or praying in other tongues, is a spiritual exercise that strengthens your inner man. Just as barbells build up your arms, praying in tongues will build up your spirit. If you'll do it faithfully, it will help bring you to the point where your spirit will be able to keep that fleshly body of yours in line.

"Well, Gloria," you may ask, "why can't I just do that by praying in English?"

Because the Bible says your "weakness" gets in the way. Many times your natural mind doesn't have the first idea how to pray as it needs to. It may not know how to pray prayers that will strengthen you against temptations that are about to come your way. Your mind is not informed as your spirit is. Your spirit is in contact with God. Let's look at Romans 8:26-28 again, this time in *The Amplified Bible:*

> The (Holy) Spirit comes to our aid and bears us up in our weakness; for we do not know what prayer to offer nor how to offer it worthily as we ought,

but the Spirit Himself goes to meet our supplication and pleads in our behalf with unspeakable yearnings and groanings too deep for utterance. And He who searches the hearts of men knows what is in the mind of the (Holy) Spirit...because the Spirit intercedes and pleads [before God] in behalf of the saints according to and in harmony with God's will.

Last session we talked about how praying in the spirit enables you to pray the perfect will of God for your life. It allows you to step out of the realm of the flesh and into the realm of the spirit so that no matter how weak or ignorant you may be in the natural, you can pray exactly as you need to.

Is it any wonder that speaking in tongues has undergone such persecution? The devil hates it! He knows it's the only way believers can pray beyond what they know.

He understands (even if we don't) that even baby Christians, newly reborn, can pray in tongues, get the mind of the Spirit, and start growing fast. That's the way the church at Jerusalem grew in the early days, you know. That's all they had. They couldn't turn to the book of Ephesians or the book of Colossians. They just had to use the ability and understanding the Holy Spirit had given them. And when they did, they turned the whole world upside down.

Let me tell you something. This will turn your world upside down too. Or, it might be more accurate to say, it will turn it right side up. It will pump you up and enable you to walk in the power of the Spirit instead of the weakness of the flesh.

But be warned, it won't work for you unless you put it to work. The Holy Spirit is a gentleman. He's not going to come storming in and make you pray in the spirit. He's going to wait on you to decide to do it. He's going to wait for you to put your will in gear.

What happens if you don't? You won't be prepared when trouble comes.

Living Prepared

In Luke 21:36, Jesus says, "Watch ye therefore, and pray always, that ye may be accounted worthy [or, as *The Amplified Bible* says, 'that you may have the full strength and ability'] to escape all these things that shall come to pass."

If you want to have the strength and ability to come through troubled times in triumph, you'd better spend some time in prayer.

That's what Jesus urged Peter and the other disciples to do in the garden of Gethsemane. He knew they were about to face one of the toughest times of their lives. He said, "Watch ye and pray, lest ye enter into temptation. The spirit truly is ready, but the flesh is weak" (Mark 14:38).

But the Scripture tells us they didn't obey Him. They slept instead. And, in Peter's life in particular, we can see the result. When temptation came, he entered into it and denied The LORD.

You may as well face it. Temptation is going to come to you as long as you live in a flesh body. So you'd better be prepared by spending some time praying in the spirit before it comes.

If you've spent much time with The LORD at all, these instructions probably don't come as much of a surprise to you. In fact, I strongly suspect that God has already been speaking to you about spending more time praying in the spirit.

I remember when He first began to speak to me about the importance of it. I'd been asking Him to show me how to quit living my life so much on the natural, circumstantial level and start walking in the spirit. *Pray an hour or two a day in the spirit* was the first instruction He gave me.

I'd been committed to The WORD for years at that time. I regularly spent much time reading and meditating on it—and that alone had already revolution-ized my life. But I knew there was still something lacking.

What God showed me was that it was time to add to The WORD by praying more in the spirit. It's really so simple, I'm surprised I didn't see it before. First Corinthians 14:14 says, "If I pray in an unknown tongue, my spirit prayeth." So when I began to pray more in tongues, I began to give my spirit more outflow. I gave vent to it.

Giving vent to your spirit is the way you walk in the spirit, just as giving vent to your flesh is the way you walk in the flesh. The more I released my spirit through tongues, the more it began to take charge. And I found it worked just as the Bible says: "Walk in the spirit, and ye shall not fulfil the lust of the flesh" (Galatians 5:16). I found it easier to hear and obey my spirit indwelt by the Holy Spirit.

Simple, isn't it? But the devil has tried to hide the simplicity of it from us be-cause he knows if we ever start doing it he'll have no place left. You see, he's limited. He can't touch your reborn spirit. The only thing he has to work on is your flesh. Once you learn what brings the flesh under dominion—that praying in the spirit applies spirit to flesh and causes the flesh to obey God the way it should—the devil won't be able to get a foothold in your life at all!

The Benefit of Revelation

But listen, the benefits of praying in tongues don't stop there. In fact, that's just the beginning! Listen to what the Apostle Paul wrote about it: "For he that speaketh in an unknown tongue speaketh not unto men, but unto God: for no man understandeth him; howbeit in the spirit he speaketh mysteries" (1 Corinthi-ans 14:2).

What are mysteries? Mysteries are things we don't know. We don't just auto-matically know, for example, what the perfect will of God is for our lives. We don't know exactly what part we've been called to play in the Body of Christ. We don't know exactly what steps to take and what moves to make each day to fulfill the plan God has laid out for our lives.

And no one in the world can tell us! As 1 Corinthians 2:9-10 says, "Eye hath not seen, nor ear heard, neither have entered into the heart of man, the things which God hath prepared for them that love him. But God hath revealed them unto us by his Spirit!"

"But how can all those things be revealed to me if I'm praying in a language I don't understand?"

They can't. That's why the Bible tells us to pray that we may interpret (1 Corinthians 14:13). As you begin to pray in the spirit, ask God to give you an understanding of what He's saying. You might not get the interpretation immediately, but eventually it will begin to bubble up inside you. You'll get an impression. A word. A sentence. Say to The LORD, "The things I don't know, teach me, and the things I don't see, show me." You'll begin to get revelation on things you've never understood before.

That's what we all need: revelation from God! You know, we're not nearly as smart as we think we are. God has things that are so far better for us than what we've seen that we can't even figure them out. But if we'll pray in the spirit, we'll get into that area out beyond our knowledge and expectation, "above all that we ask or think" as the Bible puts it (Ephesians 3:20).

I'll tell you this: If we all start praying the will of God by the power of the Spirit, this age is going to come to an end quickly! God will be able to get mysteries into the earth. He'll be able to use our mouths and authority to call forth His plan in the earth.

And, praise God, every one of us—from the least to the greatest—can participate because it's so simple! Every one of us can pray in tongues every day if we choose. You don't even have to be smart to do it. But without a doubt, if you'll do it, it will one day prove to be the smartest thing you ever did!

Daily Reflection

Why is it important to speak only words that agree with what you desire?

_____

_____

How can you stop doubt?

_____

_____

_____

What weakness does everyone face?

What are some additional benefits of praying in tongues?

Today's
Prayer of Faith

LORD, today I approach You confidently, without a doubt that what You say, You will do. Thank You that as I fill my heart and mouth with Your WORD and pray in the spirit, I am filled with Your strength and wisdom to do Your perfect will. In Jesus' Name. Amen!

Real-Life Testimonies
to Help Build Your Faith

Big Blessings

Last month, I sent a prayer request concerning a job for my daughter. Within a week she heard from the company. She was expecting an offer between $43,000 and $45,000. Well, the offer came in at $53,000! It was a fast and *big* answer to prayer.

Sovereign V.
Virginia

Chapter Five
Praying With Authority

Today, you'll discover:

The authority found in the Name of Jesus

The power that backs the Name of Jesus

How to put your angels to work in your behalf.

The Name of Jesus
by Kenneth Copeland

As a believer developing your prayer life, like it or not, you've become involved in spiritual warfare. The problems we face are brought about by satanic forces—principalities, powers, rulers of the darkness of this world and wicked spirits in heavenly places (Ephesians 6:10-18). Our responsibility is to use the weapons of our warfare to fight the good fight of faith. One of those mighty weapons for spiritual warfare is the Name of Jesus.

Every believer has the privilege of using the Name of Jesus in prayer. When you pray in Jesus' Name, you immediately get the ear of God. At the same time, you also get Satan's attention.

The Name of Jesus carries ultimate authority in the spirit world. Philippians 2:9-10 says, "God also hath highly exalted him, and given him a name which is above every name: That at the name of Jesus every knee should bow, of things in heaven, and things in earth, and things under the earth." In Jesus' Name, the believer has authority to "tread on serpents and scorpions, and over all the power of the enemy" (Luke 10:19). Satan knows the power invested in that Name and he will retreat when it is spoken in faith (James 4:7). *The New English Bible* says, "Stand up to the devil and he will turn and run"[1]!

Let's look at Hebrews 1:3-4: "Who being the brightness of his glory, and the express image of his person, and upholding all things by The WORD of his power, when he had by himself purged our sins, sat down on the right hand of the Majesty on high; being made so much better than the angels, as he hath by inheritance obtained a more excellent name than they." If the Name of Jesus is more excellent than that of the angels in good standing with God, how much more would it be than the name of Satan? He is a fallen angel!

Before He ascended into heaven, Jesus commissioned His disciples to go into all the earth. He said, "All power has been given to me in heaven and in earth. Therefore, you go into all the world. In My Name lay hands on the sick and they will recover. In My Name cast out devils." (See Matthew 28:18-19; Mark 16:17-18.) Just as a wife has power of attorney to use her husband's name, we have been given Jesus' Name to use in combat against Satan. We have authority to speak His Name in His stead.

---

1 *The New English Bible, New Testament*, Oxford University Press, 1961

When Peter and John ministered to the man at the gate Beautiful, they spoke in the Name of Jesus. Peter said, "Silver and gold have I none; but such as I have give I thee: In the name of Jesus Christ of Nazareth rise up and walk" (Acts 3:6). Later he explained what had happened. Peter said,

> Ye men of Israel, why marvel ye at this? or why look ye so earnestly on us, as though by our own power or holiness we had made this man to walk? The God of Abraham, and of Isaac, and of Jacob, the God of our fathers, hath glorified his Son Jesus.... And his name through faith in his name hath made this man strong, whom ye see and know: yea, the faith which is by him hath given him this perfect soundness in the presence of you all (Acts 3:12-13, 16).

Peter was simply using the authority Jesus had given him only a few days before. The early apostles did not have special power in themselves to do mighty works. Their holiness didn't make them special. They didn't even have the written New Testament. All they could do was speak the Name of Jesus in faith and the Holy Spirit did the mighty works. The fabulous, earthshaking revival of the early Church was sparked by only one commandment: "Go in the Name of Jesus." The power invested in Jesus' Name has never changed.

Carrying Out the Power

Most believers know that it is the Name of Jesus that caused them to be saved. The Bible says, "Whosoever shall call upon the name of The LORD shall be saved." He is rich unto those who call upon His Name (Romans 10:12-13). When you call upon someone's name, you are placing a demand on their ability. For instance, when a policeman says, "Halt in the name of the law!" he is being backed by the power of that particular city. It is as if the entire corporate structure of that city is speaking. He is carrying out the power behind the name of the law.

To know how much confidence you can place in a name, you must be able to measure the power behind it. A man writing a check places a demand on his own name. If he has the proper funds in the bank, then there is enough power to meet the demand.

The power backing the Name of Jesus is the power of Almighty God Himself! First John 3:22-23 says, "And whatsoever we ask, we receive of him, because we keep his commandments, and do those things that are pleasing in his sight. And this is his commandment, That we should believe on the name of his Son Jesus Christ, and love one another, as he gave us commandment."

Believe the Love

We have a commandment to believe on the Name of the Son of God. To believe in His Name is to put demand on His ability. Jesus said, "Whatsoever ye shall ask the Father in my name, he will give it you" (John 16:23). The mighty, powerful Name of Jesus is available to you. Become aware of your right and privilege to use it. Ask the Holy Spirit to engrave the reality of it in your heart. His ministry is to lead you into all truth (John 16:13).

The Name of Jesus is the key to heaven's storehouse. It can do anything Jesus can do. Speaking His Name is standing in His stead. According to Philippians 2:9-11, the entire spectrum of existence—heaven, earth, under the earth—will bow its knee and confess with its mouth that Jesus is Lord to the glory of God the Father. The Name of Jesus is the Name that is above every name. When He was raised from the dead, Jesus inherited the very Name of God (Hebrews 1:4). To measure the power behind His Name, you would have to measure the power of Almighty God. It can't be done. His power is measureless, and He wants to use it in our behalf.

God's love motivates Him to use His power. First John 4:16 says, "And we have known and believed the love that God hath to us...." When you believe the love He has for you, you'll begin to realize you have as much right to use the Name of Jesus as anyone else. Believe the love God has for you.

Once you recognize the reality of God's love in your life, you will realize He has not left you defenseless and powerless against evil. God covered the entire spectrum of Satan's existence with the power invested in the mighty Name of Jesus. When you pray, use it freely and confidently in the face of your adversary!

Today's Connection Points

⊙ Worship CD: "Our God" (Track 5)

If God is for us, who could be against us? Speak out the Name of Jesus today as you worship our God.

⊙ DVD: "Engage the Enemy" (Chapter 5)

Fight to keep what belongs to you. Gloria encourages you to never let the enemy have anything that rightfully belongs to you!

Faith in Action

Do all things—including prayer—in the Name of Jesus and His authority.

Notes:

_____

_____

_____

_____

_____

_____

_____

_____

_____

_____

_____

_____

_____

_____

_____

_____

_____

_____

_____

_____

_____

_____

_____

_____

_____

_____

_____

_____

_____

_____

_____

_____

_____

_____

_____

_____

_____

_____

_____

_____

Notes:

Your Angels at Work
by Gloria Copeland

Did you know that God put angels on this earth to work for you? Hebrews 1:14 asks, "Are they not all ministering spirits, sent forth to minister for them who shall be heirs of salvation?" The angels of God have been sent to minister for the heirs of the promise of Abraham (Genesis 17). And, according to Galatians 3:29, you and I are "heirs according to the promise!"

Angels of God have been sent to perform whatever is necessary to establish God's promise in the earth. They are assigned to administer THE BLESSING of Abraham to his seed in the current generation. Just as surely as God established His covenant with Isaac, He is obligated by His own WORD to establish His covenant with you. Galatians 3:29 says, "If ye be Christ's, then are ye Abraham's seed." Glory to God! If you have made Jesus The LORD of your life, then you are the seed of Abraham and heir to his blessing.

The angels are to administer the New Covenant (which is the fulfillment of the Old Covenant) to the heirs of promise. From Genesis to Revelation, you see the angels administering God's covenant to Abraham and his seed. Galatians 3:19 says the law was "ordained by angels." *W.E. Vine's Expository Dictionary of Biblical Words* says *ordained* is used in the sense of "administered." *Young's Analytical Concordance* shows the word *angel* to be "messenger" or "agent." Think of angels as *CIA—Covenant Inforcing Agents!* Although that is not spelled correctly, you get the idea! Angels are God's agents to see that His WORD, His covenant, is fulfilled in the earth.

Psalm 103:20-21 *(The Amplified Bible)* says angels are God's ministers to do His pleasure: "Bless The LORD, you His angels, you mighty ones who do His commandments, hearkening to the voice of His WORD. Bless (affectionately, gratefully praise) The LORD, all you His hosts, you His ministers who do His pleasure."

And what is God's pleasure? Psalm 35:27 says, "Let The LORD be magnified, which hath pleasure in the prosperity of his servant." His pleasure is your prosperity in every area of life: relationships, health, finances—*every* area. Praise God!

Hebrews 12:22 tells us that their number is innumerable. *The Amplified Bible* says, "countless multitudes of angels." Revelation 5:11, speaking of angels, says, "and the number of them was ten thousand times ten thousand, and thousands of thousands."

Hilton Sutton shared with us once that as nearly as he can figure that would be 100 trillion angels. One hundred trillion (in numbers) is 100,000,000,000,000. I believe that is enough to establish God's covenant in the earth! There is no shortage of angel power. Imagine—if there are 7 billion people on earth and they *all* got saved, we would still have more than 14,000 angels to minister to each of us. That's exciting!

The king of Syria sent horses, chariots and a great army to seize the prophet Elisha:

> When the servant of the man of God rose early and went out, behold, an army with horses and chariots was around the city. Elisha's servant said to him, Alas, my master! What shall we do? Elisha answered, Fear not; for those with us are more than those with them. Then Elisha prayed, Lord, I pray You, open his eyes that he may see. And The LORD opened the young man's eyes, and he saw; and behold, the mountain was full of horses and chariots of fire round about Elisha (2 Kings 6:15-17, *The Amplified Bible*).

The mountain was full of angels! Elisha's angels were ready to enforce the covenant of God. He had enough angels to take care of a "great army." There is no shortage of angels.

For the most part, the heirs of the promise have not been using the angel power available to them. There are so many angels that you are certain to have more than enough to get the job done, no matter what you exercise faith for in The WORD of God. God is able and mighty to perform His WORD! You do the believing, and God will do the performing. You believe, and God *will* establish!

The angels of God have been assigned to you as an heir of the promise. Their assignment is to establish God's promise to Abraham in your circumstances and life. In short, they are to prosper you as they prospered Abraham.

No Shortage of Angels

See yourself in this situation: You have 10,000 to 100,000 men (just natural men) working to prosper you. If these men work only eight hours a day at no charge to you, how long do you think it would take them to make you wealthy? Of course, you would have to be willing to let them work and not hinder them from fulfilling their assignments. Well, if a multitude of men operating in the natural could make you prosperous, what can the angels of God do who operate in the supernatural wisdom of God? God has made provision for us that is beyond our comprehension.

Ephesians 3:20 speaks of our God as "Him that is able to do *exceeding* abundantly above all that we ask or think, according to the power that worketh in us." God has promised to multiply Abraham's seed *exceedingly* and to be a God to them. We have been delighted just to receive what we have asked for, but according to this, God has covenanted and is able to do much, much more than we can ask or think!

I believe in these last days that we are going to rely on our inheritance of Abraham's blessing and exceed our natural thinking. If you are the seed of Abraham, all that is required of you to enjoy the covenant provisions is obedience to God's WORD. These provisions became yours through faith in Jesus Christ (Galatians 3:22). "Know therefore that The LORD thy God, he is God, the faithful God, which keepeth covenant and mercy with them that love him and keep his commandments to a thousand generations" (Deuteronomy 7:9).

Years ago, we made the decision to be obedient to God's WORD and we have prospered. But today, I have decided to go beyond all limits and allow God to multiply me exceedingly. I am an heir to His promise! You can continue to limit God if you want to, but I am willing to be blessed exceedingly beyond what I can ask or think (and I am very good at asking and thinking!).

I am believing God to establish His covenant with me in my generation. I am *willing* to receive THE BLESSING of Abraham in my time. I will not limit God to what I can ask or think. I release my faith to walk in the *exceeding* portion of the promise. I stagger not at the promise of God through unbelief. I am fully persuaded that what He has promised, He is also able to perform (Romans 4:20-21). This establishes my part of receiving.

Putting Your Angels to Work

So how do you put your angels to work in prayer? By using words. Words put angels to work on your behalf to bring to pass whatever you say. The words of your mouth bind them or loose them to work for you. If you speak faith words enforced by God's WORD, your angels are free to bring about what you want to come to pass. "Bless The LORD, you His angels, you mighty ones who do His commandments, hearkening to the voice of His WORD" (Psalm 103:20, *The Amplified Bible*). When you keep God's WORD in your mouth, you keep your angels working to bring to pass whatever you say.

The angels are waiting on your words. Even in the Old Covenant, the angel told Daniel, "thy words were heard, and I am come for thy words" (Daniel 10:12). Daniel's words put the angel to work for him. Of course, our angels are freer to work now than in Daniel's day because Jesus defeated Satan. Satan does not have the authority he had before Jesus stripped him of all his power and authority. The angels have already been sent. They are not going back and forth as Jacob saw them. They have been sent to minister for those who are heirs. They are here *now*! (Hebrews 1:14).

The moment you exercise faith in your covenant, the angels go to work to minister to you the result of your faith. They are capable spiritual beings that excel in strength. You cannot see them work. You cannot tell how much they have accomplished on your behalf, but you can believe God's WORD and know that they are doing their job. Their job is to minister for you 24 hours a day. They are not doing anything else. If you will speak God's WORD and speak only the words you want to come to pass, the angels will work for you constantly!

What authority is found in the Name of Jesus?

_____

_____

_____

What power backs the Name of Jesus?

_____

_____

_____

What do angels do?

_____

_____

_____

_____

How do you put your angels to work for you?

_____

_____

_____

_____

_____

Notes:

_____

_____

_____

_____

_____

_____

_____

_____

_____

_____

Today's

Prayer of Faith

Father God, today I stand in the Name of Jesus, speaking Your words and words of faith that send my angels to accomplish the work my words put into place. Thank You that the enemy's authority over me is broken! Praise God!

Real-Life Testimonies
to Help Build Your Faith

Praying With Authority

I had become ill the morning of Oct. 12, with a horrible runny nose and sinus congestion, and had been vomiting all day and into the night. I could not get out of bed. I awakened the next day and began to get sick again. Finally, I could no longer take the pain and illness. I was dehydrated and thought I'd need to go to the hospital. I had used three boxes of tissues blowing my nose!

So I called KCM for prayer and told the counselor my problem. She prayed that my sinuses dry up and spoke peace to my stomach. She ordered the illness to *go* in Jesus' Name and not come back. When I hung up the phone, within 30 minutes my sinuses had stopped running and my stomach was at peace. And I did not get sick again!

Karen P.
Texas

Chapter Six
Types of Effective Prayer

Today, you'll discover:

How to pray the prayer of agreement

How to pray the prayer of binding and loosing

How to pray the prayer of petition

The meaning of united prayer

The meaning of the prayer of dedication and worship

The meaning of the prayer of committal.

Kinds of Prayer I
by Kenneth Copeland

God's WORD instructs us to "pray always with all prayer" (Ephesians 6:14, 18). Other translations say, "all kinds of prayer" or "different kinds of prayer." *The Amplified Bible* says, "with all [manner of prayer]." There is more than just one kind of prayer, and depending on what you desire from The LORD, you need to understand the importance of each one. Let's discuss each of them in the light of God's WORD.

In this session, we'll look at the prayer of agreement, the prayer of binding and loosing, and the prayer of petition and supplication.

The Prayer of Agreement

When prayed according to Matthew 18:18-20, the prayer of agreement will cover every circumstance in life:

> Verily I say unto you, Whatsoever ye shall bind on earth shall be bound in heaven: and whatsoever ye shall loose on earth shall be loosed in heaven. Again I say unto you, That if two of you shall agree on earth as touching any thing that they shall ask, it shall be done for them of my Father which is in heaven. For where two or three are gathered together in my name, there am I in the midst of them.

Let me use finances to illustrate. The first thing is to agree with The WORD. Read the scriptures and pray. Gloria and I sometimes write down our agreements like this:

"We hereby agree, according to Philippians 4:19 and Matthew 18:19 as follows: 'Father, we see in Your WORD that You will supply all our needs according to Your riches in glory. We are setting ourselves in agreement that our financial need is met according to Your WORD. We believe we receive (be specific)_____. We establish this agreement, in Jesus' Name. Amen.'"

Amen means "So be it." As far as we are concerned, the matter is closed. We just thank God from that point forward. We know if we want results *we must not waver*. To waver is to doubt.

If Satan brings doubt, we simply speak to him in the authority of Jesus' Name and say, "Don't bring us your lies. Not only is it written in God's WORD, but we have agreed. We have written it down." As far as we are concerned, the need is met. There is no doubt about it because we have agreed according to The WORD of God. Consequently, our confession and actions will be in line with what we have established as truth.

I challenge you to write down your agreements. Seeing it on paper in black and white will make a difference! You will be more likely to line up your confession and actions with your agreement.

Jesus said that if any two on earth agree, He would be in the midst of that agreement to see that it comes to pass (Matthew 18:19). You are on earth so you qualify. If you agree with another believer as touching anything that lines up with The WORD of God, He is there in your midst to carry it out.

Jesus wants you to agree and will see to it that it comes to pass. The WORD *agree* is translated in *The Amplified Bible* as "agree and harmonize together or make a symphony together." The WORD *symphony* caught my attention one time, so I looked it up and found that it means to use all available instruments in harmony. You must have your spirit, mind and actions in agreement with The WORD.

Agreeing spiritually is to agree with The WORD of God. Make up your mind God's WORD is true and that it will come to pass.

Secondly, be strong in your mind. That is Satan's battleground. You must control your thoughts. Writing down your agreement will be beneficial for this reason. It will keep it before your eyes so when your mind tries to change directions, you can control it with your agreement on God's WORD. Do not tie God's hands. Allow Him to work.

You have agreed, spirit and soul (mind). Then your actions must come in line. If finances are what you agreed on, expect the money to come in. This is part of being in agreement. You cannot agree in prayer about something, then act the opposite and expect it to come to pass. If you do, your actions will eventually take over your thinking.

Agreement makes prayer work. You can experience a place of agreement with God's WORD and that harmony will produce power, as you forgive and agree with another believer. You can affect governments, families and the lives of others. You can change your financial situation and affect your church and pastor with the power of prayer. Find someone who can agree with you according to The WORD of God.

The Prayer of Binding and Loosing

God intends for the Body of Christ to police the evil forces of this world. We are to change circumstances to line up with God's will and put Satan under our feet through the power of God. We are to spoil his plans, plots and maneuvers against God's people!

The prayer of binding and loosing halts Satan's activities. Matthew 12:29 says,

"Or else how can one enter into a strong man's house, and spoil his goods, except he first bind the strong man? and then he will spoil his house." You have authority over Satan (Luke 10:19). You exercise it with the prayer of binding and loosing. "Verily I say unto you, Whatsoever ye shall bind on earth shall be bound in heaven: and whatsoever ye shall loose on earth shall be loosed in heaven" (Matthew 18:18).

As you enforce the authority vested in the Church, speak directly to Satan. Exercise your faith in Jesus' work at Calvary.

When Jesus was raised from the dead, He stripped Satan of his authority over mankind. That authority has been delegated to the Body of Christ in the earth. Bind Satan in the Name of Jesus.

Many times Gloria and I add a paragraph to our agreement prayer: "Satan, we bind you and render you helpless in this situation. As a matter of record, you are hereby bound in the Name of Jesus." From then on, we thank God that Satan is bound and unable to work in the situation. We refuse to give him any place.

The Prayer of Petition and Supplication

The words *petition* and *supplication* can be defined as "a formal request addressed to a higher power." This prayer changes things. It is based on Philippians 4:6: "Be careful for nothing; but in every thing by prayer and supplication with thanksgiving let your requests be made known unto God."

To illustrate, suppose you obtained an audience with the governor of your state. After you went through the proper channels, would you then enter his office without being prepared? Of course not! You would have your ideas formulated and the arguments settled in your mind long before you obtained an audience with him. Shouldn't you handle yourself in the same way when approaching God? Hebrews 4:16 says, "Let us therefore come boldly unto the throne of grace...."

Do not go into the prayer of petition and supplication without knowing what you want to say and how you want to say it. Enter the throne room with your petition drawn up according to God's WORD. Ask yourself these questions: What happened at Calvary? How did the substitutionary sacrifice of Jesus affect this trial I am facing? Then, find out what God has already done regarding your situation. If you need healing, look up those scriptures pertaining to healing. Present your petition. No matter what your situation may be, God has provided an answer for it in His WORD. The Cross paid the price for your deliverance.

Read the Quick Start Guide at the beginning of this LifeLine kit for an example of exactly how the Prayer of Petition and Supplication works. In the next session, we'll look at three more kinds of prayer.

Today's
Connection Points

- **Worship CD: "Agnus Dei" (Track 6)**

  He reigns! Prepare for prayer today by worshiping The LORD with all your heart.

- **DVD: "Grant" (Chapter 6)**

  Kenneth shows how to write out your needs and desires, then present them to The LORD.

Faith in Action

Pray purposefully today, selecting the type of prayer best fit for making a change in your situation.

Notes:

_____

_____

_____

_____

_____

_____

_____

_____

_____

_____

_____

_____

_____

_____

_____

_____

_____

_____

_____

_____

Notes:

Kinds of Prayer II
by Kenneth Copeland

As we learn about the different kinds of prayer, in this session we'll cover united prayer, the prayer of dedication and worship, and the prayer of committal.

United Prayer

In this day and time, united prayer is seldom discussed. Very little is taught from The WORD about praying together out loud. In many of our churches today, someone usually leads in prayer, but in most instances we see in the Bible involving a body of believers, we find them praying in a united manner. Acts 4:21-31 is the basis for united prayer. Take a moment to grab your Bible and read this passage now. Peter and John had been arrested and appeared before the religious council. Their lives were threatened if they continued to preach in the Name of Jesus. They went back to their own company and told everyone what had happened. When the people heard, they *all* prayed. A tremendous amount of power is released in united prayer.

What were the results of this prayer? Acts 5:12 says, "And by the hands of the apostles were many signs and wonders wrought among the people...." Their one request was answered exactly the way they prayed. The political system of the day tried, but could not stop the power of God in operation. This united prayer was offered accurately according to The WORD of God.

As the Body of Christ, we need to get in one accord on The WORD of God and expect results. It will cause things to change!

The Prayer of Dedication and Worship

Then cometh Jesus with them unto a place called Gethsemane, and saith unto the disciples, Sit ye here, while I go and pray yonder. And he took with him Peter and the two sons of Zebedee, and began to be sorrowful and very heavy. Then saith he unto them, My soul is exceeding sorrowful, even unto death: tarry ye here, and watch with me. And he went a little farther, and fell on his face, and prayed, saying, O my Father, if it be possible, let this cup pass from me: nevertheless not as I will, but as thou wilt (Matthew 26:36-39).

The prayer of dedication and worship holds a tremendous amount of power. We need to know how it works and when it is to be used. In the past, it has been misunderstood. When the leper came to Jesus and said, "I know You can make me well…if You will," Jesus said, "I will." He already knew the Father's will was healing. He didn't have to pray, "If it be Thy will." God's will is to be done on earth as it is in heaven (Matthew 6:9-10). Heaven has no sickness.

The only time the word "if" would *not* be an expression of unbelief is in the prayer of dedication and worship. All other times, using the word "if" in prayer can create unbelief. Praying for healing then, whether it be yours or someone else's, is a prayer that changes things, so don't use "If it be Thy will."

Unbelief hinders prayer. Most people pray, "If it be Thy will," thinking they are being humble. Actually, they are praying in ignorance of The WORD of God.

The prayer of dedication is getting your will in line with God's will to bring success into a situation. It joins you and God, and aims you toward the same goal. So many times people are running in the opposite direction of God's will, hoping God will support their endeavors. You should get God involved with your endeavors before you ever move! Never be afraid to yield your will to God. He wants you to succeed! His will is always to your advantage. When you find out what God wants you to do and you get over in it, that's where your life is going to be heaven on earth. Proverbs 16:3 in *The Amplified Bible* says, "Roll your works upon The LORD [commit and trust them wholly to Him; He will cause your thoughts to become agreeable to His will, and] so shall your plans be established and succeed."

When you pray the prayer of dedication and live by it, you will experience the peace of God because you are truly trusting Him. Isaiah 26:3 says, "Thou wilt keep him in perfect peace, whose mind is stayed on thee: because he trusteth in thee."

The Prayer of Committal

The Prayer of Committal is when you purposely commit something to The LORD—once and for all. As an example, if you will practice what I am about to share with you, this will be the last day you will ever have a worried thought. You can commit yourself and all the cares and worries of your mind to Him and enjoy divine peace.

God is vehemently against worry. It does not produce anything but stress, strain and death. Jesus preached against it. Paul preached against it. The whole Bible is against worry because Satan designed it.

Take Philippians 4:6-7 as a command. "Be careful for nothing; but in every thing by prayer and supplication with thanksgiving let your requests be made known unto God. And the peace of God, which passeth all understanding, shall keep your hearts and minds through Christ Jesus." *The Amplified Bible* says, "Do not fret or have any anxiety about anything." First Peter 5:6-7 says, "Humble yourselves therefore under the mighty hand of God, that he may exalt you in due time. Casting *all* your care upon him...." Not 75 percent of your care. Not every-thing but your kids or everything but your finances. Your confession every morn-ing should be, "I do not have a care, because it has been cast over on my Lord." Cast out every worried thought that would trample its way into your thinking. Roll it over onto Him.

Let's say you were standing about 20 feet away from me and I tossed my car keys to you. If someone else were to come to me and say, "Brother Copeland, I need the keys to your car. I need to use it." I would say, "I can't help you. I cast my keys over on him. I don't have them." I didn't say those keys ceased to exist, nor that he could not have them. I didn't say I couldn't get them back. If I went to get them, you would give them back to me. But if someone wants the car keys, they will have to talk to you because I cast them over on you.

That's what we need to do with our cares. We must cast them over on The LORD and not take them back! If Satan brings a worried thought to your mind, say-ing, *What if...*, you can tell him to talk to God about it. It is in His hands, not yours!

Many people want God to supernaturally remove their worry. But that's not the way to get the peace of God. God's peace comes by acting on His WORD that says to cast all of your worry and anxiety over on Him. You must replace those thoughts with The WORD. Philippians 4:8 says to think on "whatsoever things are true...honest...just...lovely...of good report; if there be any virtue, and if there be any praise, think on these things."

You are the one who must control your mind. The WORD says the peace of God will garrison and mount guard over your heart and mind (Philippians 4:7, *The Amplified Bible*). But you are going to have to do something. You must keep your thoughts under control.

Second Corinthians 10:5 says, "Casting down imaginations, and every high thing that exalteth itself against the knowledge of God, and bringing into captiv-ity every thought to the obedience of Christ." People have told me they can't quit worrying. They can! Anyone can stop worrying. The verse before that says the weapons of our warfare are not carnal, but powerful through God to the pulling down of strongholds. The strongholds of Satan are in the mind. He makes sug-gestions like, "It won't work this time," and "What if..." and, "But...."

The power of God begins to operate when you cast your care over on Him. As long as you worry about it, you only hinder the flow of His power and tie His hands.

Meditate on these three scriptures: 1 Peter 5:6-7; 2 Corinthians 10:5; Philip-pians 4:6. Joshua 1:8 says if you will meditate in The WORD day and night, you will be able to see how to do it. Philippians 4:9 says, "Those things, which ye have both learned, and received, and heard, and seen in me, do...." As you give your attention to these scriptures, the Holy Spirit will reveal this truth to you and you will then be able to act on it!

Philippians 4:13 is the finale: "I can do all things through Christ which strengtheneth me." You don't have to worry again.

The Greater One dwells in you. He is able to put you over. Commit to it. You will never worry again.

That's how the prayer of committal works—whether it's for worry or another area of your life you want to submit to Him.

What is the prayer of agreement?

_____

_____

What is the prayer of binding and loosing?

_____

_____

What is the prayer of petition?

_____

_____

What is united prayer?

_____

_____

_____

What is the prayer of dedication and worship?

_____

_____

_____

What is the prayer of committal?

_____

_____

_____

_____

Notes:

Today's
Prayer of Faith

Father, I come to You, in agreement with Your WORD that You supply all my needs. Your WORD is Your will, and when I pray in faith according to Your WORD, I believe what I pray will come to pass. In Jesus' Name. Amen.

Real-Life Testimonies
to Help Build Your Faith

A Christmas Prayer

On September 13, our lives were blessed with the birth of our grandson, Jaydon—an answer to his sister Ally's prayers (and certainly ours).

A few weeks before last Christmas, my 10-year-old granddaughter Ally told me she wanted a baby brother for Christmas. I laughed and told her that Nana could not do anything about that request, but she could pray about it. She did.

On January 25, our daughter Krissy called to tell me that she had not been feeling well and had taken a pregnancy test, which was positive. The pregnancy was a shock since she had not been able to get pregnant for many years. A few weeks after the pregnancy was confirmed, Krissy remembered Ally's Christmas request and called me. I heard Krissy in the background asking Ally if she had prayed for a baby brother, which was very funny because I heard Ally reply so matter of factly!

Ron W.
Kentucky

Chapter Seven
Praying for Change

Today, you'll discover:

The power of the prayer of intercession

Why intercession is considered the highest expression of love

The two types of fasts and how they differ

What fasting changes.

The Prayer of Intercession

by Kenneth Copeland

The prayer of intercession is prayed in behalf of others. Through His WORD, God has called the Body of Christ to the ministry of intercession. First Timothy 2 begins, "I exhort therefore, that, first of all, supplications, prayers, intercessions, and giving of thanks, be made for all men…." Because of the crucial time in which we are living, this move of the Holy Spirit is causing believers everywhere to respond to the call to intercession.

Why are we called to intercession? Because God does not do anything in the earth without the cooperation of a man or woman of God. He intends that we work together with Him to accomplish His will. Man is still in authority in the earth. God put him in that position.

Isaiah 59:16-17 is a great place to start our study on the art of intercession: "And he saw that there was no man, and wondered that there was no intercessor: therefore his arm brought salvation unto him; and his righteousness, it sustained him. For he put on righteousness as a breastplate, and an helmet of salvation upon his head; and he put on the garments of vengeance for clothing, and was clad with zeal as a cloak." What is "His arm"? Jesus. The sole purpose of Jesus' coming to the earth was to be that intercessor. He wore the helmet of salvation and the breastplate of righteousness. That is the same armor in Ephesians 6 for the Body of Christ.

Jesus came as an intercessor. We are to put on that same armor and enter into the same field of prayer. His arm is bringing salvation again. As intercessors, we are His arm in the earth causing reconciliation between men and God. Jesus said, "As my Father hath sent me, even so send I you" (John 20:21). The armor is the same and the calling is the same.

You may say, "Do you mean to tell me that I have the same calling on my life Jesus had?" Absolutely! Second Corinthians 5:18 says we have been given the ministry of reconciliation. Jesus said, "[You] go…into all the world, and preach the gospel to every creature" (Mark 16:15). He also said, "The works that I do shall [you] do also; and greater works than these shall [you] do; because I go unto my Father" (John 14:12). He went, didn't He? Then you and I are responsible for the works. He provided us with the new birth. God said in Ezekiel 36:26 that He would put a new spirit within us. Jesus said in John 14:17 that His Spirit would be in us. That gives us the right and the miraculous power to enter into the intercessory prayer ministry.

The Highest Expression of Love

Intercession is the highest expression of love. It is loving in the spirit, applying spiritual power for another person. It will overpower the evil influences that have bound that person. Your prayer may be for salvation, healing, or any other area of deliverance from Satan.

Second Corinthians 4:3-4 says, "But if our gospel be hid, it is hid to them that are lost: in whom the god of this world hath blinded the minds of them which believe not, lest the light of the glorious gospel of Christ, who is the image of God, should shine unto them."

Satan has blinded the minds of those who have not received the gospel. Your intercessory prayer wrestles against evil spirits that have deceived them. It is literally giving yourself, your time, your life for others. Jesus said, "Greater love hath no man than this, that a man lay down his life for his friends" (John 15:13). This is the God kind of love. It is unselfish. The world did not know this kind of love until Jesus came to the earth. He laid down His life to come to earth and live as a man. He emptied Himself of His divine privileges and fulfilled His earthly ministry as a man, filled with the Holy Spirit.

Philippians 2:7-8 says Jesus "made himself of no reputation, and took upon him the form of a servant, and was made in the likeness of men: And being found in fashion as a man, he humbled himself, and became obedient unto death, even the death of the cross." Love motivated God to send Him. "For God so loved the world, that he gave his only begotten Son, that whosoever believeth in him should not perish, but have everlasting life" (John 3:16). Jesus' love for the Father impelled Him to obey. He said, "My meat is to do the will of him that sent me, and to finish his work" (John 4:34).

Jesus has provided reconciliation between God and man through His substitutionary sacrifice at Calvary. We are co-laborers with Him. Redemption was bought with a high price. Jesus didn't take it lightly and neither should we. God's heart was hungry for a family. Jesus freely gave Himself for this desire. What an act of love!

God's heart is still hungry. He yearns for every sinner to be restored to Himself through the new birth, and every believer to be in close fellowship with Him.

To give your life means to give everything. Jesus came as an intercessor and He is still giving Himself in intercession today. Hebrews 7:25 says, "…he ever liveth to make intercession." We have said, "Jesus *gave* His life for us." But, He is still giving His life for us, still interceding. His Body in the earth is wearing the same prayer armor He wore. We have inherited His armor to do His work and enter into His ministry of intercession.

We have been given that same love that motivated Jesus to come as the intercessor! Romans 5:5 says the love of God has been shed abroad in our hearts by the Holy Ghost. The love that desires to lay down its own desires, and to intercede for someone else, is abiding on the inside of us! The love that impelled Jesus to go to the cross compels us to intercede. We pray for others so they can come into the knowledge of the truth.

Through the knowledge of God's WORD, we realize His love is in us. That love urges us to reach out to others. It urges us to be soul winners. A soul winner is an intercessor in action. Jesus paid the price to win souls. Intercessory prayer softens people's hearts to receive the message of the gospel.

Your First Assignment

Your first prayer assignment is not for yourself. It is to pray for all men, for kings and men in high authority (1 Timothy 2:1-4). When you respond to the call of intercession, the Holy Spirit prays the perfect will of God through you.

Separate yourself from the things of this world. Get in your prayer closet alone with God and commit to intercession. Begin praying for a specific body of people: a family, a village, a country, a state or a nation. You do not need to wait for a burden for this. The WORD says Jesus was moved with compassion (Matthew 9:36). Compassion is not a feeling, it is a Person. Yield to His love inside you. All the motivation you need will come that way. The One who ever liveth to make intercession is living in you! He's already motivated! Yield to Him.

Isaiah 64:7 says, "And there is none that calleth upon thy name, that stirreth up himself to take hold of thee...." The Spirit of God will not be able to help you intercede unless you are willing to stir yourself and take that position of intercession. Paul told Timothy to stir up the gift that was in him (2 Timothy 1:6). You stir it up!

Begin to pray by making yourself available to the Holy Spirit. Again, yield to Him. Allow Him to use you to pray for the man who does not have anyone to pray for him. Stand in the gap for him. Start where you are and allow it to spread to the world. You are literally fighting spiritual warfare in their behalf. The Apostle Paul said, "For I would that ye knew what great conflict I have for you, and for them at Laodicea, and for as many as have not seen my face in the flesh" (Colossians 2:1). This was the same conflict Paul talked about in Ephesians 6 when he said we don't wrestle against flesh and blood, but against principalities, powers, rulers of the darkness of this world, and spiritual wickedness in high places (Ephesians 6:12). The family of God is not based on selfishness. It is based on love. Intercession is the highest expression of love.

When you commit yourself to pray for those who need Jesus, remember the Bible says you are going to have to bind Satan in order to spoil his house (Matthew 12:29). You are confronting all the forces of evil that have them bound. Do not stop just because it looks like they will never receive. Your intercession is placing pressure on Satan and his forces. Do not relent, but persevere in prayer. It is up to them to make their own choice. But through your intercession, they will be able to make that choice. They will no longer be blinded by Satan.

Take these scriptures before the Holy Spirit and give Him the opportunity to reveal them to you personally. He is the Teacher. He can show you how they work. You can stir up the gift within you simply by desiring to know how intercession works.

This is the art of intercession. It is stirring yourself up to take hold with the Holy Spirit to cause eternal changes in the lives of others.

Today's Connection Points

(•) **Worship CD: "Welcome in This Place" (Track 7)**

Invite The LORD into your prayer time and stand, unwavering, for someone you love.

(•) **DVD: "Take It" (Chapter 7)**

Gloria reveals the word *receive* means "to take." So take everything Jesus provided for you today!

Faith in Action

Intercede for a person, family, place or nation.
Pray earnestly for them in the spirit, not letting go!

Notes:

The Fast: Releasing a Flood of Power
by Kenneth Copeland

A pipeline of God's love and power. As a born-again, Spirit-filled believer, that's what you're meant to be. When that pipeline is open and the power is flowing, you can speak with new tongues, lay hands on the sick and see them recover, preach the gospel to every creature with conviction and power, cast out devils (Mark 16:15-18) and walk in the spirit (Galatians 5:16).

But, there are times for all of us when the day-to-day business of life and the constant demands of our flesh seem to get in the way. Somehow our pipeline gets clogged with carnal things, and the rushing stream of God's power is reduced to a trickle in our lives.

It's a common problem. Even Jesus' first disciples ran into it. Jesus had given them power to cast out devils (Luke 10:19), and they had even experienced some of that power (Luke 10:17). But in Mark 9:28, we find them stumped by a particularly tough situation. They had been presented with a boy beset by a demon. And, for some reason, they found themselves unable to drive that demon out. Later, the disciples asked Jesus why they had failed. "And he said unto them, This kind can come forth by nothing, but by prayer and fasting" (verse 29).

Fasting, in this instance, would not have changed God or His will concerning the boy. But it *would* have changed the disciples. Jesus had already directed the disciples to cast the demon out. That demon was undoubtedly stubborn, and when he resisted, the disciples slipped into unbelief. Had they been fasting and praying, they would have been strong in the spirit, and they would have been able to do what Jesus did—cast the demon out! (See John 14:12.)

A Spiritual Tool

Fasting is a valuable spiritual tool. So let's look into it a little more closely. There are basically two categories of fasting. The first category is a *proclaimed fast* (Joel 1:14). A *proclaimed fast* brings you to a place where you can hear from God. The ideal time to go on a proclaimed fast is when you need divine direction.

In 2 Chronicles 20:1-15, the Bible tells what happened to God's people when they fasted and prayed to seek His direction. There we see the Israelites hemmed in by their enemies and badly in need of divine guidance. Their king, Jehoshaphat, proclaimed a fast that was directed toward seeking The LORD. He wanted to draw people's attention toward God. Why? Because God reveals Himself to people who are seeking Him, whether individually or corporately.

When the congregation was in one accord, the Spirit of The LORD came upon Jahaziel. "And he said, Hearken ye, all Judah, and ye inhabitants of Jerusalem, and thou king Jehoshaphat, Thus saith The LORD unto you, Be not afraid nor dismayed by reason of this great multitude; for the battle is not yours, but God's" (2 Chronicles 20:15). Imagine how good that sounded to their ears! The Holy Spirit spoke and that was the reward they were seeking!

The second type of fasting is a *personal fast* (Matthew 6). It also yields very gratifying rewards. In Matthew 6:16-18 Jesus said, "Moreover when ye fast, be not, as the hypocrites, of a sad countenance: for they disfigure their faces, that they may appear unto men to fast. Verily I say unto you, They have their reward. But thou, when thou fastest, anoint thine head, and wash thy face; That thou appear not unto men to fast, but unto thy Father which is in secret: and thy Father, which seeth in secret, shall reward thee openly." You can either receive your reward from the admiration of men or you can receive your reward from God. The key is fasting in secret so that God can reward you openly. Being proud of the fact that you're fasting will destroy everything you are trying to accomplish.

In Isaiah 58, God explains the kind of fast to which He is calling the Body of Christ. That passage will give you a good idea of the kinds of rewards to believe God for when you fast. There The LORD says, "Is not this the fast that I have chosen? to loose the bands of wickedness, to undo the heavy burdens, and to let the oppressed go free, and that ye break every yoke?" (Isaiah 58:6).

According to that scripture, you can fast for the deliverance of a friend or loved one—to set them free from oppression of the devil. You can fast for other believers who are under heavy burdens. And you can fast to break the yoke of bondage within your own life.

Fasting Checklist

Here is a five-step checklist for fasting that will help you put yourself in a position to receive from God spiritually. You can take these steps and order your thinking by them:

1. Decide the purpose of the fast. No matter what you are seeking from The LORD, decide before you begin what you wish to obtain through your effort. Find God's promises that cover your situation, and believe you receive before the fast begins. Faith brings the results you desire, and faith is born out of The WORD, not out of fasting.
2. Proclaim the fast before The LORD.
3. Believe you receive the reward (Matthew 6:18)—before the fast. The reward will probably be related to the first step. The purpose of the fast will have a great deal to do with the rewards involved. If you are fasting

for revelation knowledge, the reward would be receiving the knowledge you desire.

4. Minister to The LORD. "Let The WORD of Christ dwell in you richly in all wisdom; teaching and admonishing one another in psalms and hymns and spiritual songs, singing with grace in your hearts to The LORD" (Colossians 3:16). One of the best things you can do to learn how to minister to The LORD is to read the Psalms. You minister to The LORD by speaking of His mighty works. When you begin to praise and minister to Him, He will get involved with you! You need to fellowship with Him, and He needs to hear your praise and thanksgiving. I heard myself saying to The LORD one day, "Jesus, You are my High Priest. Take my praise and minister it unto my Father. Make it a sweet incense to His nostrils. Blot out all the sin that has come up before Him from this miserable planet. Minister my praise and love and adoration to Him. Cause it to be just what He needs today. I want to bless His heart. I do not want Him to be grieved by the sinfulness of man." I began to realize that my heavenly Father needs this. Earthly fathers long to hear their children tell them how much they love them instead of just begging for things. "I love you, Dad," is a statement that captures a father's heart. Just think how much that means to our heavenly Father!

5. Minister to others. Always minister to others after the fast. You need to use the spiritual power within you to meet the needs of people. If you fast according to The WORD of God, you will be spiritually built up. Minister to others during the fast only as you are led of the Father.

It is important for you to understand that it's not the fasting itself that brings the deliverance. Jesus has already obtained deliverance through the complete work of redemption. And the Holy Spirit who lives inside you knows how to pray in order to bring the deliverance Jesus has already provided. Fasting simply brings the spirit man which is in union with the Holy Spirit into ascendance over the flesh. It also limits the influence of the physical appetites so that you can more effectively hear from and respond to the Spirit. This enhances intercession, and effective, Holy Spirit-led intercession sets the captive free!

There are many rewards for fasting. You can fast for personal rewards—to tap into a greater anointing in your life and ministry. You can also fast to receive divine direction. But nothing can bring you closer to God's will than living a life of prayer and fasting.

Just remember, fasting is not a method of twisting God's arm to get Him to respond when you pray. Fasting does not change God, it changes you!

Daily Reflection

What is the prayer of intercession?

_____

_____

Why is intercession considered the highest expression of love?

_____

_____

_____

What are the two types of fasts and how do they differ?

_____

_____

_____

Who does fasting change?

_____

_____

_____

Notes:

_____

_____

_____

_____

_____

_____

_____

_____

_____

_____

_____

_____

_____

_____

_____

_____

Today's Prayer of Faith

Holy Spirit, teach me the art of intercession. Use me as Your vessel to show God's love in the earth. I yield myself to pray for those who need You. I am an intercessor!

Real-Life Testimonies
To Help Build Your Faith

A Life Changed

My son Loren prayed for Sammy—with whom he had robbed a jewelry store—to get saved. The court sent Loren to Teen Challenge instead of prison, and Loren had all of Teen Challenge praying for Sammy. This past October, Sammy got out of prison and moved back to our town. Loren, who is living now with us and is on probation, found out that Sammy accepted The LORD while in prison! Sammy grew up in Ethiopia and was raised Muslim. We praise God for this man's salvation!

Janet K.
Indiana

Chapter Eight
Thanksgiving and Praise

Today, you'll discover:

How thanksgiving and praise work with your faith

What is meant by a "sacrifice of praise"

The biblical definition of joy

How joy and praise work together.

Into His Courts With Praise

by Kenneth Copeland

Thanksgiving and praise are integral parts of prayer.

The Bible says if you pray according to God's will, you know He hears you, and you have the petitions you desired of Him (1 John 5:14-15). God's WORD is His will. You don't have to wait until you can see the manifestation before you believe you have it. If you believe you receive when you pray, you can begin to praise God for the answer.

Faith involves thanksgiving and praise. Philippians 4:6 says, "Be careful for nothing; but in every thing by prayer and supplication with thanksgiving let your requests be made known unto God."

You and God are working together. It is your prayer and His power.

Praise is more than just words. There is power in it. God did not ordain praise just so we could brag on Him. Psalm 8:1-2 says, "O Lord our Lord, how excellent is thy name in all the earth! who hast set thy glory above the heavens. Out of the mouth of babes and sucklings hast thou ordained strength because of thine enemies, that thou mightest still the enemy and the avenger." Jesus quoted this scripture and said, "Out of the mouth of babes and sucklings thou hast perfected praise" (Matthew 21:16). Strength and praise are the same according to The WORD of God. God ordained praise to stop Satan in his tracks.

Once you have believed that you have received because of The WORD, your faith is in action. Through praise, you are throwing your faith up against that mountain of adversity in your life. Jesus said if you have faith and doubt not, you can speak to the mountain and it will be removed. You will have what you say. If you quit applying the force of faith, the mountain will not be removed. You want the mountain to keep moving until it sinks into the sea and is completely out of sight! Apply the force of faith by praising God that it is gone!

Keep the Pressure On

The only way Satan can stop you and your faith is through unbelief. He does not have power to stop God. He cannot stop that mountain from moving into the sea. The only way he can succeed is to make you stop applying the pressure.

The mountain may be sickness, disease, alcohol, family trouble, financial trouble or any evil work. Jesus bought and paid for the answer to all of it. You cannot face any problem that has not been taken care of through Calvary's Cross.

The psalmist David said, "I will praise thee, O Lord, with my whole heart; I will show forth all thy marvellous works. I will be glad and rejoice in thee: I will sing praise to thy name, O thou most High. When mine enemies are turned back, they shall fall and perish at thy presence" (Psalm 9:1-3). He did not say *if.* He said *when* the enemies fall back! As you praise God, those enemies will retreat. The Bible says He inhabits the praises of His people (Psalm 22:3).

Praise is not something you just feel once in a while. God is worthy of your praise. The Bible says to offer the sacrifice of praise. What did Israel do in the Old Testament when they had problems they could not overcome? The priest would offer sacrifices to God to bring Him on the scene and God would stop the onslaught of the enemy. As a new covenant believer, you are a priest of God. No other sacrifice can be offered. Jesus offered the ultimate blood sacrifice. As a priest, you offer the sacrifice of praise. Hebrews 13:15 says, "By him therefore let us offer the sacrifice of praise to God continually, that is, the fruit of our lips giving thanks to his name."

In Luke 17, Jesus ministered to 10 men who had leprosy. They said, "Jesus, Master, have mercy on us. And when he saw them, he said unto them, Go show yourselves unto the priests. And it came to pass, that, as they went, they were cleansed" (verses 13-14). Verse 15 says, "And one of them, when he saw that he was healed, turned back, and with a loud voice glorified [praised] God." They were all cleansed. But only one praised God unashamedly. Jesus said, "Were not the ten cleansed? but where are the nine?" Then He said to the man, "Thy faith hath made thee whole" (verse 19). The others were cleansed, but he was made whole! His faith kept working. His mountain did not stop at the seashore or sink halfway into the sea! No trace of his mountain was left. Whatever the disease had destroyed was restored.

That is the kind of power you can have right now in your own life. If you are not familiar with praising God, or it makes you feel uncomfortable, ask God to show you how. You can start by reading the Psalms aloud. They speak of the great and mighty works of God. They praise Him for His goodness, power and mercy. God is faithful to perfect your praises!

Today's Connection Points

● **Worship CD: "How Great Is Our God" (Track 8)**

Enter His courts with praise, proclaiming the greatness and goodness of our God!

● **DVD: "Into Thanksgiving" (Chapter 8)**

Gloria teaches how to leave your place of prayer, acting as if it has already been answered—and thanking God for it until it appears.

Faith in Action

Give God praise for the breakthrough you've been praying for.

Thank Him for the answer!

Notes:

_____

_____

_____

_____

_____

_____

_____

_____

_____

_____

_____

_____

_____

_____

_____

_____

_____

_____

_____

_____

A Blaze of Praise:
The Secret of Supernatural Combustion

by Gloria Copeland

Praise infuses your prayers with power—especially when it's full of joy.

Some years ago, when I first began to catch sight of the supernatural power of joy, I did a study on it. During that study, I discovered that one of the biblical words for *joy* is translated "to shine."[1] Another word means "to leap."[2] Another means "to delight."[3] But in every case, joy is more than an attitude. It is an action.

As I studied, I also found out that joyful praise gives God pleasure. Psalm 149 says: "Praise ye The LORD. Sing unto The LORD a new song, and his praise in the congregation of saints. Let Israel rejoice in him that made him: let the children of Zion be joyful in their King. Let them praise his name in the dance: let them sing praises unto him with the timbrel and harp. For The LORD taketh pleasure in his people" (verses 1-4).

It doesn't offend God when we boisterously praise Him. He likes it. It gives Him pleasure to see us shine and leap and express our delight in Him.

"Let the saints be joyful in glory.... Let the high praises of God be in their mouth, and a twoedged sword in their hand" (verses 5-6).

I know that by natural standards, that kind of exuberant praise doesn't look very dignified. But as believers, we need to get past the point where we care about that. We need to focus instead on pleasing God. We should have such a desire to please Him that we don't care how we look to other people.

Your Greatest Desire

When we become like Jesus and desire God so intensely that we're willing to cast aside our desire to please men and praise Him without reserve, we'll truly see the glory of God.

Why? Because God manifests Himself where He's wanted. He shows up where hearts are hungry. He's not going to reveal Himself to a great degree among people whose hearts are partially turned to Him and partially turned toward something else.

God told Moses, "As truly as I live, all the earth shall be filled with the glory of The LORD" (Numbers 14:21). That's what He wants. He's wanted it for a very

[1,2,3]. James Strong, *The New Strong's Exhaustive Concordance of the Bible* (Nashville: Thomas Nelson Publishers, 1984) H8055, H1750, G5460, G5479, H4885

long time. But He has to have a people who will allow Him to be their God—with nothing else before Him. They have to want Him and His presence more than they want to be respected in their neighborhood. They have to want Him more than anything else life has to offer.

Today He is finding people who are willing to do that. People who literally praise God with all their hearts.

If you are one of those people, you've probably already found out that some people don't like it. The glory of God offends them, and they don't want to be around you.

Not surprisingly, very often it is the religious people who will criticize you most harshly.

After Jesus healed the blind man, the religious leaders told him, "Don't give that Jesus any credit—He's a sinner" (John 9:24, my paraphrase).

The sick, hungry people of the world won't say things like that. They're not like the people who have been "religionized." They want help, and they don't care where they get it.

They have the same attitude as the man who was born blind. He said to the Pharisees, "Whether he (Jesus) be a sinner or no, I know not: one thing I know, that whereas I was blind, now I see" (verse 25).

Now, That's Power!

If you're not sure you have the strength to face the criticism of religious people, I have good news for you. You can get that strength by rejoicing, because the Bible says, "The joy of The LORD is your strength" (Nehemiah 8:10).

Joy and praise together release strength on the inside of you and power on the outside. Psalm 9:1-3 says it this way: "I will praise thee, O Lord, with my whole heart; I will show forth all thy marvellous works. I will be glad and rejoice in thee: I will sing praise to thy name, O thou most High. When mine enemies are turned back, they shall fall and perish at thy presence."

God inhabits our praises (Psalm 22:3). And, when His presence begins to come into our midst, our enemies fall back. They can't stand the presence of God. "Let God arise, let his enemies be scattered: let them also that hate him flee before him. As smoke is driven away, so drive them away: as wax melteth before the fire, so let the wicked perish at the presence of God. But let the righteous be glad; let them rejoice before God: yea, let them exceedingly rejoice" (Psalm 68:1-3).

Now that's power! When God's people rise up in praise and worship and celebrate the victories of God, His enemies are scattered.

No wonder Satan has tried so hard to get God's people to sit still. No wonder he has bound us up with traditions that taught us to sit back in dignified silence. (The word *dignity* can mean "to be self-possessed.") For most of us, our traditions have taught us not to do the very things the Bible says we are to do when we worship and praise.

Burn, Brother, Burn!

But tradition's day is over. I'm telling you, when the Spirit begins to move, inhibition has to flee. The Bible says, "And they...shall be like a mighty man, and their heart shall rejoice as through wine" (Zechariah 10:7).

You know what happens when people drink wine—they lose their inhibitions! That's what happened to the disciples on the Day of Pentecost. They had been hiding out only days before, but when the Holy Ghost came upon them, suddenly they were out on the streets acting so wild everyone thought they'd been drinking.

Listen, what God considers "dignified" and what you consider dignified are two different things. God wants you free. He doesn't want you bound up with traditions or fear of what other people might think.

He wants you free to laugh. He wants you free to leap and praise and sing. He wants you free to rejoice. He wants you so free that other people won't understand it—they'll just want it!

Never underestimate the drawing power of joy. It's like a blazing fire that captures the attention of people in darkness. In fact, in a dream I had many years ago, God called it "spontaneous combustion."

I didn't even know what the term meant until the next day. When I looked it up in a dictionary, here's what I found: *Spontaneous combustion*—"the process of catching fire as a result of heat generated by an internal chemical reaction."[4]

That's it! Joy—the process of catching fire and burning as a result of heat which comes from the Holy Spirit.

It's time to rejoice, to rise up out of our exhaustion and implement the power of praise in our prayer life. When we do, we'll enter a domain of power, freedom and the joy of The LORD—a domain that's alive and shining with the presence of God.

So throw off those old inhibitions. Take God at His WORD. Leap. Shout. Sing. Let yourself catch fire in the Spirit, and never stop burning.

---

[4] Webster's New World College Dictionary, Forth Edition, ed. Michael Agnes, David B. Guralnik [Cleveland: Wiley Publishing Inc. 2002] "spontaneous combustion"

Daily Reflection

How do thanksgiving and praise work with your faith?

_____

_____

What is a "sacrifice of praise"?

_____

_____

What is the biblical definition of joy?

_____

_____

How do joy and praise work together?

_____

_____

_____

Notes:

_____

_____

_____

_____

_____

_____

_____

_____

_____

_____

_____

_____

_____

_____

_____

_____

_____

Today's Prayer of Faith

Father, I come to You today in the Name of Jesus with a heart full of thanksgiving for the answers You bring into my life. You always supply, and always bless me. You are truly worthy of my praise!

Real-Life Testimonies
to Help Build Your Faith

Great Thanksgiving

This is a letter of thanksgiving to you for all the prayers that were offered up on my behalf for healing from breast cancer with lymphatic involvement. After nine and a half months of treatment I was declared to be in remission. All organs were said to be clear, all scans showed nothing, and my blood tests were fine. This report could only have been possible because of the prayers of God's children like you and faith in God's promises that "by His stripes we are healed."

Again, thank you to each and every one of you who offered prayer on my behalf. We serve a living God who hears and answers prayer. Medical science calls it remission; I call it *HEALED* in Jesus' Name!

Ramona B.
Texas

Chapter Nine
Prayer Blockers

Today, you'll discover:

Some of the common hindrances to prayer

Some things that might have hindered your own prayers

How you can overcome dwelling on past failures

Why harmony in your home is so important.

Hindrances to Prayer
by Kenneth Copeland

By this session, hopefully you see clearly that God's desire is to answer your prayers. He has even given us His WORD so we can pray according to His will. Unanswered prayer is not the result of God's unwillingness to use His power, but because of hindrances we allow to overcome us. The Bible says His eyes look to and fro throughout the earth to show Himself strong in behalf of those whose hearts are perfect toward Him (2 Chronicles 16:9). When we are aware of these hindrances and how to avoid them, we will experience the joy of answered prayer.

Doubt and Unbelief

In chapter four, we talked about two of the greatest hindrances to the believer's prayer life: doubt and unbelief. I want to emphasize them again in this session and add that though doubt and unbelief are similar, there are differences. Doubt is the thief of God's greater blessings. It keeps a man in a state of separation from Him. Some men doubt there is a God or doubt He will perform His WORD in response to their prayers. As a result, they do not respond to His WORD. This hinders His power in their behalf.

Doubt comes from ignorance of God's WORD. For example, many have the idea that God will no longer heal or they think He is not interested in their financial affairs. Consequently, their prayers are hindered.

Unbelief is when a man knows there is a God, yet does not believe His WORD. He knows what the Bible says, but has chosen to believe what he can see and feel instead. This will definitely hinder his prayer life.

In order to expel doubt and unbelief, you must make God's WORD final authority in every matter, not allowing religious tradition, or what you think about the situation, to be the deciding factor. Pray according to the will of God, and believe you receive when you pray. God's WORD is His will. He does not will one thing and say another. God cannot lie. Refuse to be moved by anything except what God's WORD tells you.

When you pray, expect things to change. God's WORD will not fail.

Lack of Knowledge of Our Right-Standing With God

The second great hindrance to prayer is the lack of knowledge of our right-standing with God. Most people do not understand what God actually did in Christ Jesus at Calvary. Jesus became our sin so we could become the righteousness of God (2 Corinthians 5:21). Righteousness is right-standing with God. Your righteousness is vitally important in the field of prayer.

Your right-standing with God gives you the right to approach God in prayer without a sense of guilt, sin or condemnation. There is a confidence you experience, knowing you will receive when you ask in faith, believing.

No man on earth deserves God's righteousness. But when he receives Jesus as Lord, he is placed in right-standing with God. He is made the righteousness of God by grace through faith (Romans 3:21-23).

The WORD says God is not holding sin against the world (2 Corinthians 5:17-21). He sent Jesus to take your place. If you recognize this and let Him be your righteousness, God will answer your prayer as if Jesus Himself prayed it.

Ignorance of Our Right to Use the Name of Jesus

Lack of knowledge of our right to use the Name of Jesus is the third great hindrance to prayer. A great void of knowledge of the power in Jesus' Name exists in most Christian circles. John 16:23 says, "And in that day ye shall ask me nothing. Verily, verily, I say unto you, Whatsoever ye shall ask the Father in my name, he will give it you."

Go before the Father in Jesus' Name. You are already going before Him in Jesus' power and His faith. Your prayer will be answered.

No believer would ever doubt the *power* of Jesus' Name or that the Father hears that Name in prayer. What, then, is the problem? The root of unbelief where the Name of Jesus is concerned is in not believing we have the right to use it. *Will the Father hear me pray in that Name?*

I have a right to use my name because it was given to me by my father. He gave me the name of Kenneth Copeland. I came into the world with the right to use it. When you make Jesus Christ The LORD of your life, God becomes your Father. The Bible says any man who believes that Jesus is the Christ, is born of God (1 John 5:1). Once you realize you have the right to use the family name, you will see God's power operating mightily in your behalf.

Unforgiveness and Strife

Another hindrance to prayer is found in Mark 11:25-26. It says, "And when ye stand praying, forgive, if ye have aught against any: that your Father also which is in heaven may forgive you your trespasses. But if ye do not forgive, neither will your Father which is in heaven forgive your trespasses." This is vital. Prayer will not work without forgiveness. I cannot overemphasize its importance.

Strife and unforgiveness hinder your prayer life. Strife is merely acting on unforgiveness. James 3:16 says, "For where envying and strife is, there is confusion and every evil work." When you take confusion and add it to Satan's work, problems arise. You will have a disaster in the making. Jesus is not in the midst of that. The next time someone says something rude, unmannerly or unkind to you, or about someone else, make the decision not to join in. Don't carry strife any further.

The absence of strife is the key to getting rid of confusion and evil. It is the predominant, primary prerequisite for answered prayer.

Lack of Knowledge of Fellowship

Lack of knowledge of the value of fellowshiping with God will also hinder your prayer life. If you do not know the importance of close, intimate fellowship with God, you will not likely see results in prayer. Set apart a specific time to be alone with Him and to direct all your attention toward Him. It is easy to say, "I don't have time to stop everything else, so I'll just fellowship with God 'on the go.' If He has something to tell me, He can say it while I'm doing this or that." Yes, you can commune with God wherever you are and in whatever you are doing, but you must get quiet and spend quality time in His presence to hear His voice. When you are "on the go," you will do most of the talking.

The Bible says in 1 John 1:3-4, "That which we have seen and heard declare we unto you, that ye also may have fellowship with us: and truly our fellowship is with the Father, and with his Son Jesus Christ. And these things write we unto you, that your joy may be full." You are called into fellowship with the Father. This is why God made man in the first place—to fellowship with Him.

The Past

Finally, dwelling on past failures can hinder our prayers. Instead of putting our painful failures behind us, we often dwell on them until those failures become more real to us than the promises of God. We focus on them until we become bogged down in depression, frozen in our tracks by the fear that if we go on, we'll only fail again.

Hounded by the memory of some financial failure, we may shrink from God's promises of prosperity. Hurt by the experience of losing a loved one to disease in spite of our prayers, we may find we're suddenly afraid to believe God for healing anymore. Paralyzed by the weaknesses that have marked our past, we may be tempted to give up on the bold dreams God has given us for the future—whatever they may be.

It's a downward spiral that leads from discouragement to depression to despair. But there is a way out. The LORD revealed it to me some time ago when I was going through a period of great, great torment in my own life. I'd been through some failures and some disappointments. And, no matter what I tried to do, I couldn't seem to shake the depressing effects of them.

Then suddenly one day, The LORD spoke up inside my spirit and said, *Kenneth, your problem is you're forming your thoughts off the past instead of the future. Don't do that! Unbelief looks at the past and says, "See, it can't be done." But faith looks at the future and says, "It can be done! And, according to the promises of God, it is done!" Then, putting past failures behind it forever, faith steps out and acts like the victory has already been won.*

What I'm saying to you is this: If depression has driven you into a spiritual nose dive, all you have to do to break out of it is to get your eyes off the past and onto your future—a future that's been guaranteed by Christ Jesus through the exceeding great and precious promises in His WORD.

I know that's not as simple as it sounds on paper. But you can do it—because you are actually "a new creature." The old things of your life—the failures and disappointments—have truly passed away and all things have become new (2 Corinthians 5:17-18; Galatians 2:20)!

God remembers your iniquities no more (Hebrews 8:12), so neither should you. Instead, replace thoughts of the past with scriptural promises about your future. As you do, the spiritual aches and pains and bumps and bruises that have crippled you for so long will quickly disappear!

Today's Connection Points

● **Worship CD: "Blameless" (Track 9)**

You are blameless before The LORD. Don't allow the enemy to convince you otherwise as you worship God today.

● **DVD: "Get In Agreement" (Chapter 9)**

Strife hinders your prayers. Kenneth admonishes us to stay out of strife at all costs!

Faith in Action

Examine your life for things that might be hindering your prayers.

Take immediate action to correct them with the help of the Holy Spirit.

Notes:

Love in the Home
by Gloria Copeland

I want to talk for a moment about what Ken mentioned in this morning's connection about strife being a hindrance to answered prayer.

Ken and I have learned the importance of agreement in the home. We have learned through The WORD how to live in agreement with each other and with our children. The power of harmony is at work in our lives; whatever we agree on according to God's WORD comes to pass. We do not allow strife in our home, in our office, or in any part of our ministry. Strife stops the power of God!

We have learned a great truth: It is more important to avoid strife than to appear justified! It is better to give than to receive, and the wisdom from above is peace-loving and easily entreated, willing to yield to reason. As a result, we are enjoying one of God's greatest blessings, a love-ruled home.

When you begin to order your life by the love of God, you will find that the easiest place to remain in selfishness is in your own home with those dearest to you. There seems to be an incentive to operate in love before other people, but with your family you are tempted to allow yourself more selfish privileges—as if selfishness did not really count at home. There is no barrier in the home to keep you from seeking your own except the love of God. Before you even thought about living the love of God, you were probably more courteous and just nicer in many ways to friends and acquaintances than to your family. Without the love of God you are more demanding and less forgiving with the members of your family than with anyone else. It does not make sense, but most of the time you will say things to those close to you that you would not dream of saying to other people.

Discord or disagreement in any relationship, whether between husband and wife, parent and child or brother and sister, drops the shield of faith and stops prayer results. It invites Satan and his evil spirits into the midst of you.

Where there is envying and strife, there is confusion and every evil work (James 3:16)! Envy (jealousy) and strife (contention, rivalry and selfish ambition) are areas of darkness. Envy results in strife. Strife opens the door to every evil work and brings confusion. Your senses will dominate your spirit. Strife will stop you from perfecting the love of God and cause you to walk in darkness instead of in the light of God's wisdom.

Stop Strife Immediately

Strife is deadly. It stops faith and paralyzes the power of God in your life. The moment that you become aware of Satan trying to move you into an area of strife, stop it immediately with the Name of Jesus. Learn to resist strife just as you learned to resist sin and sickness. Stop contention. It proceeds from Satan. The WORD says, "Let nothing be done through strife or vainglory" (Philippians 2:3). Obey God's WORD and be free from Satan's evil works.

Strife and selfishness are luxuries Christians cannot afford—*especially* at home! If you allow Satan to stop you with strife at your own front door, you will be no threat to him anywhere else. The home is where strife is the deadliest, but also the place that living the love of God produces the greatest joy and blessing. When your home is love-ruled by The WORD of God, it will become a copy of heaven on earth.

A Christian husband and wife who learn to live in agreement without strife are mighty instruments of The LORD Jesus for good. The rewards of living in agreement are more than worth the effort it takes to walk in love with each other. When you're in harmony, your prayers are effective!

Daily Reflection

What are some of the common hindrances to prayer?

_____

_____

_____

What are some things that may have hindered your own prayers?

_____

_____

_____

How can you overcome dwelling on past failures?

_____

_____

_____

Why is harmony in your home so important?

_____

_____

_____

_____

Notes

Today's Prayer of Faith

Father, You have redeemed me from the darkness of this world. I refuse to allow strife, envy, jealousy, past failures, un-forgiveness or doubt to operate in my life! Please bring to light anything that would hinder my prayers so they can be fervent and effectual! In Jesus' Name. Amen.

Real-Life Testimonies
to Help Build Your Faith

Enemies Become Friends

Last month I asked for prayer for my high-school reunion. Praise God, it was a huge success. Everyone marveled at how good it was. But the thing that touched my heart the most was a classmate who had a grudge for 50 years, who made up with her "enemy." Thank you so much for your prayers. There are no small requests with our Father.

Shirley L.
South Carolina

Chapter Ten
A Lifestyle of Prayer

Today, you'll discover:

Your biblical role in standing for your nation

How Proverbs 21:1 can impact your prayer time

Which prayer principles from this LifeLine kit have had the most impact on you

What new, godly habits you can form as a result of what you have learned from using this LifeLine kit.

A Higher Form of Power
by Kenneth Copeland

As we reach the end of this LifeLine kit, we must talk about the believer's responsibility to pray for our country, because the responsibility for a nation does not rest solely on the shoulders of its politicians. It rests also in the hearts of born-again believers who've been given a higher form of power in prayer.

What I have to say to you in this session is simple, and quite serious. Your response to it will not only affect your life and mine, but thousands of others.

It is a message—no, a command—all of us have, no doubt, heard before. But most have ignored it. We have thought somehow we could get by without it, that we could let it slip without paying a price.

But we *have* paid. Our whole nation has paid. One look at any newspaper will give you an idea just how dearly.

The command I'm talking about is the one found in 1 Timothy 2:1-2. There the Apostle Paul says, "I exhort therefore, that, first of all, supplications, prayers, intercessions, and giving of thanks, be made for all men; for kings, and for all that are in authority; that we may lead a quiet and peaceable life in all godliness and honesty."

That verse is clear, isn't it? The instruction is plain. Yet even in these tumultuous days when our nation is so desperately in need of God's guidance, most of God's people don't do what that verse commands.

Why not?

Is it because we don't care? Is it because we're unwilling to invest a few minutes of prayer in the future of our nation each day?

No.

I believe it's because most of us are overwhelmed by the problems we see around us. *How could my prayers make a dent in the national debt?* we think. *How could my faith affect foreign policy?*

In other words, we fail to pray because we fail to realize just how powerfully our prayers can affect our country.

Ordained by God

Let's look at some scriptures and find out what The WORD of God has to say about this subject.

First, let's look at Romans 13:1. There, the Apostle Paul writes, "Let every soul be subject unto the higher powers. For there is no power but of God: the powers that be are ordained of God."

It amazes me how little attention is paid to this very important scripture. In fact, when you get right down to it, most Christians don't even believe it! You can tell by the disrespectful way they talk about our leaders.

"Well, if those leaders are ordained of God," you may say, "why don't they act like it?"

Because the believers they govern aren't praying for them!

You see, if by prayer we will invite God into our governments, He'll take control of those who've been put in positions of authority. As Proverbs 21:1 says, "The king's heart is in the hand of The LORD, as the rivers of water: he turneth it whithersoever he will."

Think about that for a moment! God has reserved the right to override the will of a nation's leader, if need be, to see that His people are governed according to His will.

What's more, God will hear the prayer of any government leader. Even if he's the worst reprobate in the whole world. He heard the prayer of old King Nebuchadnezzar, so that means He'll listen to any leader!

When you have time, read the account of Nebuchadnezzar in Daniel 4 because it's a powerful example of what we're talking about here.

Nebuchadnezzar was king of Babylon. He was an ungodly ruler of an ungodly nation. He'd taken captives, however, from the land of Judah. He had some of God's people under his authority. So, God began to deal with him.

God warned him, *Nebuchadnezzar, you're going to lose your mind if you don't straighten up.* But Nebuchadnezzar refused to listen. And, sure enough, he went just as crazy as could be.

He stayed that way for years, too. He ran up and down through the woods like a wild man. But one day he cried out to God, and God heard him.

Despite his status as a heathen king of a heathen nation, God intervened repeatedly in Nebuchadnezzar's life and heard him when he finally cried out for help. Why? Because Nebuchadnezzar had God's people under his control!

That same principle still holds true today. If we'll open the way through prayer, God will deal with our leaders! He'll turn the hearts of everyone from the White House on down to make sure His children are governed justly. In fact, if we'll just be obedient to 1 Timothy 2:1-2, there's no council of any kind on earth, no king, no president, no congress, no one who can overthrow God's purpose for His people.

But if we're ever going to see that happen, we're going to have to take The WORD of God and go to war in prayer and in faithful intercession.

Fighting the Fight

Unfortunately, most of us don't know the first thing about fighting this kind of war. Ephesians 6:10-12 says it's not a battle of flesh and blood, but of the spirit. In fact, let's look at those verses and see exactly what they say about this fight:

> Finally, my brethren, be strong in The LORD, and in the power of his might. Put on the whole armour of God, that ye may be able to stand against the wiles of the devil. For we wrestle not against flesh and blood, but against principalities, against powers, against the rulers of the darkness of this world, against spiritual wickedness in high places.

Read that last verse again.

Most believers are so earthly minded (or carnally minded) they never even realize where the enemy's attacks are actually coming from. They blame circumstances and people, and waste their energy fighting natural conditions instead of supernatural causes.

We need to wake up to the warfare going on in the heavenly realm!

It's time we begin to realize how important we are to world affairs. Since the day Jesus gave us the Great Commission, the life or death of the world has been in the hands of the Church. We are the ones who have the mighty Name of Jesus and the awesome strength of the gospel to bring life and abundance to every creature.

God has called us to intercede. He has commanded us to pray for those in authority. He has given us His WORD, His power, His Name, His authority and His faith. We have all the tools necessary to pray effectively for our government and its leaders.

Let's band together as never before in intercession for our country and for all the nations of the world. We are God's people, called by His Name, and we can stand in faith before God for the healing of our land.

Today's Connection Points

⊙ **Worship CD: "You Said" (Track 10)**

Stand for the nations today, speaking God's WORD, and believing for the healing of our land.

⊙ **DVD: "Pray Always" (Chapter 10)**

Gloria reminds us to walk in faith and love, spending time with God every day.

Faith in Action

🖐 *Pray for those in authority today, proclaiming that "Jesus Is Lord!" over your nation.*

Notes:

Notes:

A Deeper Life in Prayer
by Kenneth Copeland

Gloria and I believe prayer is vitally important for every child of God. For the final session in this LifeLine book, we wanted to summarize the material we've covered, sharing some necessary guidelines in the development of a deeper life in prayer. These will cause your prayer life to become accurate.

Accuracy produces results. Charles Finney wrote in one of his memorandums: "I have had some experiences in prayer of late that have alarmed me." I thought about that for a while. I realized I hadn't really had any prayer experiences that were "alarming." I made the decision to get involved in my prayer life like he did. As my prayer life deepened, I began to have some awesome experiences.

When you are accurate in your prayer life, you are operating out of your spirit rather than just your mind. Your spiritual ears are open to the voice of God. Train yourself not to make a move without listening to the Spirit of God. He is the intercessor. You are the mouthpiece. "Likewise the Spirit also helpeth our infirmities: for we know not what we should pray for as we ought: but the Spirit itself maketh intercession for us with groanings which cannot be uttered" (Romans 8:26). If you never attempt to be accurate in prayer, you will never be sure about the results. You'll just be hoping for something to happen.

Keys to Accuracy

The coming of the Holy Spirit changed the whole perspective of prayer. This is a key to accuracy. Jesus said,

> And in that day [after the Holy Spirit comes] ye shall ask me nothing. Verily, verily, I say unto you, Whatsoever ye shall ask the Father in my name, he will give it you. Hitherto have ye asked nothing in my name: ask, and ye shall receive, that your joy may be full. These things have I spoken unto you in proverbs: but the time cometh, when I shall no more speak unto you in proverbs, but I shall show you plainly of the Father. At that day ye shall ask in my name: and I say not unto you, that I will pray the Father for you: for the Father himself loveth you, because ye have loved me, and have believed that I came out from God (John 16:23-27).

Pray to the Father in Jesus' Name. Jesus endorses your prayer. With His Name, you are given free access to the throne of God. You short-circuit the system when you make your requests to Jesus. He said to pray this way: "Our Father which art in heaven, Hallowed be thy name..." (Luke 11:2). If you want Jesus to endorse your prayer, you need to pray to the Father in Jesus' Name.

Believe you receive when you pray. Mark 11:24 states, "Therefore I say unto you, What things soever ye desire, when ye pray, believe that ye receive them, and ye shall have them." *The Amplified Bible* says, "For this reason I am telling you, whatever you ask for in prayer, believe (trust and be confident) that it is granted to you, and you will [get it]." Note the word *granted*. John 16:23 in *The Amplified Bible* says, "And when that time comes, you will ask nothing of Me [you will need to ask Me no questions]. I assure you, most solemnly I tell you, that My Father will grant you whatever you ask in My Name...." *To grant* means "to bestow possession of by title or deed." You need no other evidence than God's WORD. Believe you receive. Learn to do this every time you pray, and learn to pray with your Bible open. Don't major on the problem. Start with the answer. Be specific when you pray. God said He would watch over His WORD to perform it (Jeremiah 1:12). Once you are involved in His WORD, He can work for you. Be fully persuaded that God can perform His WORD for you (Romans 4:21).

Forgive. Your faith will not work accurately in an unforgiving heart. Jesus commanded us to forgive (Mark 11:24-25). Your prayers will not work effectively with sin in your life. The promises won't work without meeting the conditions. All you have to do is confess unforgiveness. He is faithful and just to forgive you and cleanse you from all unrighteousness. Keep your prayer life exact by keeping sin out of your life. Keep the forgiveness door to your heart open. Maintain fellowship with your Father.

Depend on the Holy Spirit in your prayer life. Romans 8:26 says: "Likewise the Spirit also helpeth our infirmities: for we know not what we should pray for as we ought: but the Spirit itself maketh intercession for us with groanings which cannot be uttered." The Holy Spirit is your helper, standby, teacher, strengthener, comforter, intercessor and counselor. Depend on Him when you pray. Operate in faith instead of by feeling.

Staying in Tune

Allow the spirit realm to become a reality to you. Purpose to see beyond the realm of your five physical senses. Remember, you are a spirit. You have a soul. You live in a body. Your body is just the "earth suit" for your spirit. It is not the real you.

Many people want to see visions or an angel appear. Seeking after something you can see with your natural eye or hear with your natural ear is the lowest form of spiritual manifestation. If you are not in tune with God spiritually, you would not be able to understand a vision if you saw one. When you become spiritually in tune, you do not need confirmation from your senses. The WORD is enough evidence. God will confirm His WORD to you when you are in faith (Mark 16:20). Rely on the Holy Spirit.

Learn to pray for others. First Timothy 2:1 says, "I exhort therefore, that, first of all, supplications, prayers, intercessions, and giving of thanks, be made for all men." Train yourself to do this first of all. The result of praying for others is that you live a quiet and peaceable life in all godliness and honesty. Anytime the Church of Jesus Christ is in turmoil, its members are not praying for others.

The Apostle Paul said spiritual maturity demands that each believer does his part (Ephesians 4:15-16). Verse 16 says, "From whom the whole body fitly joined together and compacted by that which every joint supplieth, according to the effectual working in the measure of every part, maketh increase of the body unto the edifying of itself in love." Each part has a contribution to make to the rest of the Body. We are to supply to one another as we draw from God through our fellowship with Him.

As you become involved with intercessory prayer for the Body of Christ, the whole operation will begin to be successful. When you pray and supply the things that cause the Body to be compacted together, Satan cannot tear it down. Pray the prayer of intercession. It will cause us to come together in unity.

I suggest you set up a time and place to pray the prayer of intercession—even if it is just for five minutes. It will grow into 10 minutes, 15 minutes, 20 minutes and so on. Your intercession has a positive effect on the lives of others.

Praying in the Spirit

Spend time praying in the spirit. Jude 20 says, "But ye, beloved, building up yourselves on your most holy faith, praying in the Holy Ghost." Take the time to pray daily in other tongues specifically for edification. It will draw you into a deeper life in prayer and will keep you prepared at all times. First Corinthians 14:4 says, "He that speaketh in an unknown tongue edifieth himself." The word *edify* translated in the Greek means the same as "charging a battery."

Praying in other tongues will keep you tuned in to the Spirit. It will help you overcome the weakness of your flesh.

God needs a Church that is not walking after the flesh. As we walk in the spirit and sow to the spirit, we stay "charged" and ready to do battle in the spirit! God needs each of us in this critical time.

Always base your prayer on The WORD of God. Prayer based on The WORD is based on God's will. God's WORD is His will. James 4:3 says, "Ye ask, and receive not, because ye ask amiss...." If you pray according to God's WORD, you cannot ask amiss. All Scripture is profitable for correction and instruction (2 Timothy 3:16). When you pray in line with God's WORD, you can have the confidence that your prayers are free from error.

You can have a deeper life in prayer!

Daily Reflection

What is your biblical role in standing in faith for your nation?

_____

_____

What does Proverbs 21:1 mean when it states, "The king's heart is in the hand of The LORD, as the rivers of water: he turneth it whithersoever he will"?

_____

_____

What prayer principles from this LifeLine kit have hit home most to you?

_____

_____

What new, godly habits can you form in your life today from what you have learned in this LifeLine kit?

_____

_____

_____

Notes:

_____

_____

_____

_____

_____

_____

_____

_____

_____

_____

_____

_____

_____

Today's Prayer of Faith

Heavenly Father, today is the beginning of my deeper life of prayer. I know now that You answer prayer, and I desire an effectual, fervent prayer life. Help me stay committed and disciplined. I want to seek You and know You. You said in John 10:27, "My sheep hear my voice, and I know them, and they follow me." You are my Good Shepherd, and I thank You, Lord, that You lead me, and I hear Your voice. I am listening, Lord! In Jesus' Name. Amen.

Real-Life Testimonies
to Help Build Your Faith

Let the Reconciliation Begin

I've had you praying for our son who walked away from his family 10 years ago. On October 4, I called and left a Happy Birthday message on his phone. He called me the next day and thanked me. Let the reconciliation begin! Praise Jesus, and thank you for your prayers.

Marilyn B.
Arizona

In what areas has your faith grown the most from your use of the LifeLine materials?

_____
_____
_____
_____
_____
_____
_____
_____
_____
_____
_____

Name some ways you are putting your faith into action right now?

_____
_____
_____
_____
_____
_____
_____
_____
_____
_____

What are ways you can be a blessing to others this week?

_____
_____
_____
_____
_____
_____
_____
_____
_____
_____

Appendix A
Prayers and Confessions
Based on God's Word

These can also be found on your Faith in Action Cards.

1. 1 Thessalonians 5:17; Luke 18:1

I will pray without ceasing. Yes, I will always pray and not faint!

2. Romans 7:6 (The Amplified Bible); Hebrews 3:15

I serve You, Lord, with joy and gladness of heart in obedience to the promptings of the Holy Spirit. Thank You that I hear Your voice, and I determine to obey and not harden my heart.

3. 1 John 5:14-15

This is the confidence that I have in The LORD: That if I ask anything according to His will (His WORD), He hears me. And since I know He hears me, whatever I ask, in faith, I receive.

4. Mark 11:24

Whatever things I desire, when I pray, I believe that I receive them—and I shall have them.

5. 1 John 3:22-23

Whatever I ask the Father according to His WORD, in Jesus' Name, He will give me.

6. Ephesians 6:18

I pray always with all kinds of prayer and supplication in the spirit.

7. Hebrews 7:25; Romans 5:5

Jesus ever lives to make intercession for me—and His love is shed abroad in my heart by the Holy Spirit. Therefore, I live to intercede for others, too.

8. Philippians 4:6; Psalm 149:6

In everything by prayer and supplication with thanksgiving, I let my requests be made known to God. The high praises of God are in my mouth and the two-edged sword of The WORD in my hand.

9. Romans 5:5

I live in forgiveness and confidence because the love of God is shed abroad in my heart by the Holy Spirit.

10. 1 Timothy 2:1-2

I pray and intercede first of all, for all men, for kings and all who are in authority, that I may lead a quiet and peaceable life in all godliness and honesty.

Appendix B
Prayers for Specific Situations

Prayer based on The WORD is already in line with the will of God. First John 5:14-15 tells us that we know God hears us and answers our prayer when we ask according to His will. The following prayers have been compiled from The WORD of God on various subjects. They will aid you in getting your prayer life off to a good start.

To Make Jesus The LORD of Your Life

Do you know where you stand with God?

If you have never made Jesus The LORD of your life, then you are separated from God through sin. God loves you so much He gave His only begotten Son for you. You are the reason He sent Jesus to the cross. John 3:16 says, "For God so loved the world, that he gave his only begotten Son, that whosoever believeth in him should not perish, but have everlasting life." Second Corinthians 5:21 says God made Jesus, who knew no sin, to be sin for us. Jesus is the spotless Son of God. He knew no sin, but God made Him to be sin for us. Sin was the reason Jesus came to earth. He died on the Cross and went to hell for one reason: to pay the price for sin. Once that price was paid, Jesus was raised from the dead, triumphant over Satan, and the sin problem was taken care of.

God is not holding your sin against you. He sent Jesus as your substitute. He paid the debt. Now you can receive the credit for what He did in your place (Isaiah 53:3-5).

The price has been paid, but it's not an automatic thing. You must choose to accept what He did for you and receive Him as your personal Savior. If you have never done so, choose Him now. Repent of your sin (turn totally from it) and pray this prayer. When you do, the power of God will make you a new creation in Christ Jesus. Say:

> Heavenly Father, in the Name of Jesus, I present myself to You. I pray and ask Jesus to be Lord over my life. I believe it in my heart, so I say with my mouth that Jesus has been raised from the dead. This moment, I make Him The LORD over my life. Jesus, come into my heart. I believe this moment that I am saved. I say it now: I am reborn. I am a Christian. I am a child of Almighty God!
>
> *Scripture References:* John 1:12, 3:16, 6:37, 10:10, 14:6, 16:8-9; Romans 3:23, 5:8, 10:9-10, 13; 2 Corinthians 5:17, 19, 21.

To Be Filled With the Holy Spirit

After Jesus Christ was raised from the dead and before He ascended into heaven, He left us this promise: "Ye shall receive power, after that the Holy Ghost is come upon you: and ye shall be witnesses unto me...[throughout] the earth" (Acts 1:8). The Holy Spirit is the One who endues us with power for our Christian walk and to do the works of Jesus (John 14:12).

God has already sent the Holy Spirit. He came to earth on the day of Pentecost (Acts 2). Now it is up to you to receive Him into your life.

Once you are born again, you can receive the power of the Holy Spirit just as you received Jesus—by faith in God's WORD. All you must do is ask Him. Jesus said, "If ye then, being evil, know how to give good gifts unto your children: how much more shall your heavenly Father give the Holy Spirit to them that *ask* him?" (Luke 11:13). The Holy Spirit will empower you with God's own power! You need His power working in you—ask Him now.

> My heavenly Father, I am a believer. I am Your child, and You are my Father. Jesus is my LORD. I believe with all my heart that Your WORD is true. Your WORD says that if I will ask, I will receive the Baptism in the Holy Spirit, so in the Name of Jesus

Christ my LORD, I am asking You to fill me to overflowing with Your precious Holy Spirit. Baptize me in the Holy Spirit. Because of Your WORD, I believe that I now receive, and I thank You for it. I believe that the Holy Spirit is within me and, by faith, I accept it. Now, Holy Spirit, rise up within me as I praise my God. I fully expect to speak with other tongues as You give me the utterance.

Meditate on these scriptures about the Holy Spirit: Luke 11:9-13; John 14:10, 12, 16-17; Acts 1:8, 2:4, 32-33, 38-39, 8:12-17, 10:44-46, 19:2, 5-6; 1 Corinthians 14:2-15, 18, 27; Ephesians 6:18; Jude 20.

Salvation in Behalf of Others

Father, I come before You in prayer and in faith, believing. Your WORD says You desire for all men to be saved and to come into the knowledge of the truth, so I bring _____ before You this day.

I break the power of Satan from his assignments and activities in _____'s life in the Name of Jesus. Now, while Satan is bound, I ask that You send forth the perfect laborers to share the good news of the gospel in such a way that he/she will listen and understand it. As the truth is ministered, I believe _____ will come to his/her senses and come out of the snare of the devil and make Jesus The LORD of his/her life.

Father, I ask that You fill _____ with the knowledge of Your will in all wisdom and spiritual understanding. As I intercede in his/her behalf, I believe that the power of the Holy Spirit is activated and from this moment on, I will praise and thank You for _____'s salvation.

I am confident that You are alert and active, watching over Your WORD to perform it. It will not return to You void. It will accomplish that which You please, and prosper in the thing whereto it was sent. Therefore, my confession of faith is, "God has begun a good work in _____'s life, and He will perform it and bring it to full completion until the day of Jesus Christ. In Jesus' Name. Amen.

Scripture References from *The Amplified Bible:* 2 Peter 3:9; Matthew 18:18, 9:37-38; 2 Timothy 2:26; Jeremiah 1:12; Isaiah 55:11; Philippians 1:6.

A Harmonious Marriage

Father, in the Name of Jesus, it is written in Your WORD that love is shed abroad in our hearts by the Holy Ghost who is given to us. Because You are in us, we acknowledge that love reigns supreme.

We believe that love is displayed in full expression, enfolding and knitting us together in truth, making us perfect for every good work to do Your will, and working in us that which is well-pleasing in Your sight.

We desire to live and conduct ourselves and our marriage honorably and becomingly. We esteem it as precious, worthy and of great price. We commit ourselves to live in mutual harmony and accord with one another, delighting in each other, being of the same mind and united in spirit.

Father, we believe and say that we are gentle, compassionate, courteous, tenderhearted and humble-minded. We seek peace and it keeps our hearts in quietness and assurance. Because we follow after love and dwell in peace, our prayers are not hindered in any way in the Name of Jesus. We are heirs together of the grace of life.

We purpose together to live in agreement, to live in harmony, to live in peace, to live in power toward each other and toward all men. We confess that our marriage grows stronger day by day in the bond of unity because it is founded on Your WORD and rooted and grounded in Your love. Father, we thank You for the performance of it in Jesus' Name.

Scripture References: The Amplified Bible: Romans 5:5; Philippians 1:9; Colossians 3:14, 1:10; Philippians 2:2, 13; Ephesians 4:32; Isaiah 32:17; Philippians 4:7; 1 Peter 3:7; Ephesians 3:17-18; Jeremiah 1:12.

Your Children

Father, Your WORD is true and I believe it. Therefore, in the Name of Jesus, I believe in my heart and say with my mouth that Your WORD prevails over my children. Your WORD says You will pour out Your Spirit upon my offspring, and Your BLESSING upon my descendants. I believe and say that my children are wise, they take heed to and are the fruit of godly instruction and correction. I love my children and I will diligently discipline them early. Because of that, they give me delight and rest.

Father, I take Your WORD that says You contend with him who contends with me and You give safety to my children and ease them day by day. I confess that You, Lord, give Your angels special charge over my children to accompany and defend and preserve them. I believe they find favor, good understanding and high esteem in Your sight, LORD, and in the sight of man.

I confess that my children are disciples, taught of You, LORD, and obedient to Your will. Great is their peace and undisturbed composure. I believe I receive wisdom and counsel in bringing up my children in Your discipline and instruction. Your WORD declares that when they are old they will not depart from it. So, I commit them into Your keeping and I know, and have confident trust, that they are watched over and blessed of You all the days of their lives, in Jesus' Name.

Scripture References: The Amplified Bible: Mark 11:23; Isaiah 44:3; Proverbs 13:1, 24, 29:17; Isaiah 49:25; Psalm 91:11; Proverbs 3:4; Isaiah 54:13; Proverbs 2:6; Ephesians 6:4; Proverbs 22:6; Deuteronomy 28:6. Also see Deuteronomy 28:13; Psalm 127:3-5; Isaiah 55:11; Jeremiah 1:12.

When Desiring Children

Father, we desire to have a baby, and since Your WORD says that children are a gift from You, we expect to have a normal, healthy baby. Since _____ has been redeemed from the curse, we expect her to carry that child full term. Your WORD says You will bless the fruit of her womb, that she will lose none of her young by miscarriage or be barren, and that You will keep her safe through childbearing. Since she is no longer under the curse, _____ will be able to have this child the way You originally planned for Eve to have children—free from pain and suffering and pangs and spasms of distress. So we expect this child to be brought into the world quickly and with no pain. We believe she will feel the contractions but no pain. We believe, according to Your WORD, that she will have a beautiful pregnancy with no suffering.

Thank You, Father, for hearing and answering our prayers and for faithfully watching over Your WORD to perform it. We know You have given Your angels charge over us to accompany and defend and preserve us in all our ways.

Now, Satan, you hear The WORD of God. We speak it to you and command you to take your hands off us, God's children, in the Name of Jesus. We break all assignments you have put up against us and forbid you to hinder this pregnancy or childbirth in any way. The WORD of God declares that whatever we bind on earth is bound in heaven, and whatever we loose on earth is loosed in heaven. So we bind you, now, in Jesus' Name. And we loose the peace of God to flood our hearts.

Thank You, LORD, for hearing and answering our prayers. We love and appreciate You and look forward to seeing this precious little love that You have especially picked out for us!

Scripture References: Psalm 127:3; Galatians 3:13; Psalm 139:13, 91:11; Isaiah 49:1, 55:11; Matthew 16:19.

Walking in the Perfect Peace of God

Father, in Jesus' Name, I thank You that Your peace is my covenant right in Christ Jesus. I will keep my mind fixed on You, trust in You, and You will keep me in perfect peace.

I will not fret or have anxiety about anything, but in every circumstance and in everything by prayer and petition with thanksgiving, I will continue to make my wants known to You, Father. And Your peace, which transcends all understanding, shall garrison and mount guard over my mind and heart in Christ Jesus. I fix my mind only on that which is true, worthy of reverence, honorable, just, pure, lovely, kind and gracious. If there is anything worthy of praise, I will think on and weigh and take account only of these things.

I will let Your peace rule in my heart. As I do, I believe my calm and undisturbed heart and mind are life and health to my physical body. I humble myself under Your mighty hand, casting all my concerns and anxieties on You, once and for all, because I know You care for me affectionately and about me watchfully.

I thank You, Father, that You have not given me a spirit of timidity, of cowardice, of craven and cringing and fawning fear. The spirit I have from You is the spirit of power, love, a calm and well-balanced mind, and of discipline and self-control. You, LORD, are on my side. I will not fear. What can man do to me? You are my light and my salvation. Whom shall I fear or dread? You, LORD, are the refuge and stronghold of my life; of whom shall I be afraid? I love Your law, O LORD. Nothing shall offend me or make me stumble. I walk in great peace, in Jesus' Name. Amen.

Scripture References: Isaiah 26:3; *The Amplified Bible:* Philippians 4:6-8; Colossians 3:15; Proverbs 14:30; 1 Peter 5:6-7; 2 Timothy 1:7; Psalms 27:1, 118:6, 119:165.

Walking in the Wisdom and Guidance of the Holy Spirit

Father, in the Name of Jesus, I realize that as a believer, my body is the temple of the Holy Spirit. My acknowledgment of Your presence on a daily basis makes my faith in You effectual. I believe that You, heavenly Father, are leading and guiding me by the Holy Spirit through my spirit, and illuminating my mind.

As I yield to the Holy Spirit, I believe that my steps are ordered of You, LORD. I commit and trust myself wholly to Your guidance, expecting You to cause my thoughts to become agreeable to Your will, so my plans will be established and succeed. I trust in You, LORD, with all my heart and lean not on my own understanding. As I acknowledge You, You direct me in paths of righteousness.

I confess that as I become more God-inside minded, I can more easily recognize the inward witness of the Holy Spirit. I hear the voice of the Good Shepherd, and a stranger's voice I will not follow. I am aware that my spirit is the candle of The LORD.

I meditate in The WORD day and night, not letting it depart from my mouth. I test my inward witness with The WORD, for the Spirit and The WORD agree. I am quick to act on The WORD, as well as the prompting of my spirit. I am not a hearer only, but also a doer. Therefore, I am blessed in all my deeds.

Scripture References: 1 Corinthians 6:19; Philemon 6; John 16:13; Romans 8:14; Psalm 37:23; Proverbs 16:3, 3:5-6; Psalm 23:3, *The Amplified Bible;* Romans 8:16; John 10:5, 27; Proverbs 20:27; Joshua 1:8; 1 John 5:7; James 1:25.

Spiritual Growth

Heavenly Father, I cease not to pray for _____, that You may grant him/her a spirit of wisdom, revelation and insight into mysteries and secrets in the deep and intimate knowledge of You. I pray that the eyes of his/her heart are flooded with light so that he/she can know and understand the hope to which You have called him/her, and to know how rich Your glorious inheritance is in the saints.

I pray that _____ walks, lives and conducts himself/herself in a manner worthy of You, fully pleasing to You and desiring to please You in all things, bearing fruit in every good work and steadily growing and increasing in the knowledge of You. I pray that he/she may be invigorated and strengthened with all power by Your Spirit to exercise every kind of endurance and patience, perseverance and forbearance with joy.

I believe the good work You began in _____ will continue, right up to the time of Jesus' return, perfecting it and bringing it to its full completion in him/her, in Jesus' Name. Amen.

Scripture References: The Amplified Bible: Ephesians 1:17-19; Colossians 1:10-11; Philippians 1:6.

Spiritual Insight

Father, in the Name of Jesus, I bring _____ before You today. I take authority over Satan and bind his operation in _____'s life. Now, I ask You to send the perfect laborers into his/her path to minister The WORD of faith to him/her. I pray that the eyes of his/her understanding may be enlightened that he/she may know how rich is Your inheritance in the saints, that _____ may be filled with the knowledge of Your will in all wisdom and spiritual understanding, walking fully pleasing to You, increasing in the knowledge of God.

Father, I pray that _____ will be rooted and built up in Jesus, established in faith. I am confident that He which began a good work in _____'s life will continue until the day of Jesus Christ.

I know You've heard my prayer, so I know that I have the petitions that I ask. Thank You, in Jesus' Name. Amen.

Scripture References: Matthew 9:38; Ephesians 1:16-18; Colossians 1:9-12, 2:6-10; Philippians 1:6; 1 John 5:14-15.

Health and Healing

Father, in the Name of Jesus, I confess Your WORD concerning healing. I believe and say that Your WORD will not return to You void, but will accomplish what it says it will. Therefore, I believe in the Name of Jesus, that I am healed according to 1 Peter 2:24. It is written in Your WORD that Jesus Himself took my infirmities and bore my sicknesses (Matthew 8:17). Therefore, with great boldness and confidence, I say on the authority of that written WORD that I am redeemed from the curse of sickness, and I refuse to tolerate its symptoms.

Satan, I speak to you in the Name of Jesus and say that your principalities, powers, master spirits who rule the present darkness and your spiritual wickedness in heavenly places are bound from operating against me in any way. I am loosed from your assign-ment. I am the property of Almighty God and give you no place in me. I dwell in the secret place of the Most High God. I abide, remain stable and fixed under the shadow of the Almighty, whose power no foe can withstand.

Now, Father, because I reverence and worship You, I have the assurance of Your WORD that the angel of The LORD encamps around about me and delivers me from every evil work. No evil shall befall me, no plague or calamity shall come near my dwelling. I confess The WORD of God abides in me and delivers to me perfect sound-ness of mind and wholeness in body and spirit from the deepest parts of my nature in my immortal spirit, even to the joints and marrow of my bones. That WORD is medica-tion and life to my flesh, for the law of the Spirit of life operates in me and makes me free from the law of sin and death.

I have on the whole armor of God. The shield of faith protects me from all the fiery darts of the wicked. Jesus is the High Priest of my confession, and I hold fast to my confession of faith in God's WORD. I stand immovable and fixed in full assurance that I have health and healing *now* in the Name of Jesus.

Scripture References: Isaiah 55:11; Galatians 3:13; Ephesians 6:12; 2 Corinthians 10:4; James 4:7; Psalms 91:1, 34:7, 91:10; Hebrews 4:12, *The Amplified Bible;* Proverbs 4:20-22; Romans 8:2; Ephesians 6:16; Hebrews 4:14; Psalm 112:7.

Finances

Heavenly Father, I have chosen Jesus as The LORD of my life and I seek first Your kingdom and Your righteousness, believing that the material things I need will be supplied. I choose for my character and moral disposition to be free from the love of money, greed, lust and craving for earthly possessions. I am satisfied with my present circumstances and with what I have, being confident because You have promised You will not in any way fail me, nor leave me without support. I am confident in Your faithfulness, that You will never leave me nor forsake me, nor leave me helpless.

I take comfort and am encouraged. I boldly say that The LORD is my helper and I will not be seized with alarm. I will not fear, dread or be terrified.

I believe, Father, that You wish above all things that I prosper and be in health even as my soul prospers. I will meditate in Your WORD day and night, not letting it depart from my mouth, keeping it in the midst of my heart, observing to do all that is written therein. I believe then I shall make my way prosperous and have good success. You have promised that as a doer of The WORD I will be blessed in all my deeds. I am assured that You will withhold no good thing from me as I walk uprightly. The uncompromising are never forsaken. I make it my ambition to live quietly and peacefully. I will mind my own affairs, working with my hands so that I may bear myself becomingly, correctly and honorably, and command the respect of the outside world, being self-supporting, dependent on no one and having need of nothing.

Knowing through Your WORD, Father, that You are The LORD my God who teaches me to profit and who leads me by the way I should go, I will put Your principles to work in my life regarding employment. I choose to apply myself to good deeds—to honest labor and honorable employment—so that I may be able to meet necessary demands whenever the occasion may require, and that I may not live an idle, uncultivated, unfruitful life, in Jesus' Name.

I labor so that I may walk honestly toward those who are without. As I give, it is given to me again—good measure, pressed down, shaken together and running over. I do not sow sparingly and grudgingly, but rather, I sow generously, blessing others. Therefore, I can expect to reap generously and with blessings.

Scripture References: Matthew 6:33; Hebrews 13:5-6, *The Amplified Bible;* 3 John 2; Joshua 1:8; Psalm 84:11; James 1:25; 1 Thessalonians 4:11-12, *The Amplified Bible;* Isaiah 48:17; Titus 3:14, *The Amplified Bible;* 1 Thessalonians 4:12; Luke 6:38; 2 Corinthians 9:6.

Employment

Father, in Jesus' Name, I seek Your wisdom and trust You to direct me in seeking the job that is best for me. I will walk in mercy and truth and lean not unto my own understanding. Thank You for opening wide a door which no man can shut and for giving me favor.

It is my desire, Father, to be debt free and owe no man anything except to love him, according to Your WORD. I am willing to work with my own hands, so that I lack nothing. I praise You that it is Your will that I am self-sufficient financially and have an abundance to meet all of my needs, with enough left over to give generously to others.

I will not fret or have anxiety about anything, Father, for Your peace mounts guard over my heart and mind. Because You are my source, I have confidence, comfort and encouragement in Your provision. I thank You, Father, for supplying my need of employment according to Your riches in glory by Christ Jesus.

Scripture References: Proverbs 3:3-5; Revelation 3:8; Psalm 5:12; Romans 13:8; 1 Thessalonians 4:11-12; 2 Corinthians 9:8, *The Amplified Bible;* Philippians 4:6-7, *The Amplified Bible;* 2 Corinthians 1:3, *The Amplified Bible;* Philippians 4:19.

Overcoming Bad Habits

Father, I believe that my faith becomes effectual—divinely energized—by the acknowledging of every good thing which is in me, in Christ Jesus. Through my union with Christ, I am a new creature. Old things are passed away and all things have become new.

I was crucified with Christ, nevertheless I live; yet not I, but Christ lives in me. I was buried with Him in baptism, and raised together with Him by the power of the Holy Spirit so that I might habitually live and behave in newness of life. My old, unrenewed self was nailed to the Cross with Him in order that my body, which is the instrument of sin, might be made ineffective and inactive for evil and that I might no longer be the slave of sin.

Just as death no longer has power over Jesus Christ, neither does sin have dominion over me, through my union with Him. I consider myself dead to sin and my relation to it broken. I am alive only to God, living in unbroken fellowship with Him, in Christ Jesus.

I have been delivered from the control and dominion of darkness and transferred into the kingdom of light. I have been raised together with Christ and am seated together with Him, far above principalities, powers, rulers of the darkness of this world and wicked spirits in high places. Sin shall no longer exert dominion over me, but I have dominion over sin. It is under my feet, in the Name of Jesus. Amen.

Scripture References: Philemon 6; 2 Corinthians 5:17; Galatians 2:20; Romans 6:4, 6, 10-11, 14; Colossians 1:13, *The Amplified Bible;* Ephesians 1:21, 2:6, 6:12.

Protection

Father, in the Name of Jesus, I thank You that You watch over Your WORD to perform it.

Father, I praise You that I dwell in the secret place of the Most High and that I shall remain stable and fixed under the shadow of the Almighty—whose power no foe can withstand. I will say of You, Lord, "The LORD is my refuge and my fortress, my God; on Him I lean and rely, and in Him I confidently trust!"

For then You will deliver me from the snare of the fowler and from the deadly pestilence. Then You will cover me with Your feathers, and under Your wings shall I trust and find refuge. Your truth and Your faithfulness are a shield and a buckler.

Father, You are my confidence, firm and strong. You keep my foot from stumbling, being caught in a trap, or hidden danger. Father, You give me safety and ease me. I know You will keep me in perfect peace because my mind is stayed on You, and I trust in You. I thank You, LORD, that I may lie down and You will give me peaceful sleep, for You sustain me and make me dwell in safety.

I shall not be afraid of the terror of the night, nor of the arrow (the evil plots and slanders of the wicked) that flies by day, nor of the pestilence that stalks in darkness, nor of the destruction and sudden death that surprise and lay waste at noonday.

A thousand may fall at my side, and 10,000 at my right hand, but it shall not come near me. Only a spectator shall I be—inaccessible in the secret place of the Most High—as I witness the reward of the wicked.

Scripture References: Jeremiah 1:12; Psalms 91:1-16, 112:7, *The Amplified Bible;* Proverbs 3:26, *The Amplified Bible;* Proverbs 3:23-24; Psalms 3:5, 4:8, 127:2, 34:7.

When Involved in Court Cases

Father, I ask You to help me as I face this legal battle. I thank You for being a very present help in time of trouble. I open my heart to the Holy Spirit to reveal any of my own disobedience in this matter so that I may repent and receive Your forgiveness. Deliver me from hate and revenge.

In the Name of Jesus, I ask You to cause truth to prevail. Thank You for protecting me from lying tongues and deceitful lips. I believe and declare that no weapon formed against me will prosper, and any tongue unjustly rising against me will be shown to be wrong. I dwell in Your secret place, which hides me from the strife of tongues. I thank You that false witnesses who speak against me will be caught in their own trap. Thank You for helping me as I reply in defense. I believe Your Spirit gives me the words to say when I need them.

By an act of my will, I refuse to fear, and I cast down any imagination that tries to exalt itself above the knowledge of You and Your love.

In the Name of Jesus, I now cast the care of this court case upon You. I resist anxiety, and receive calmness and peace. I believe Your favor and the favor of man will surround me like a shield.

Your WORD says You perfect that which concerns me, so I make a conscious decision to receive Your perfected end in this case. I give You all the glory for all that will be accomplished, and I will testify of Your goodness. Amen.

Scripture References: Genesis 15:1; Exodus 4:15, 14:13; Deuteronomy 3:22, 20:3, 31:6, 8; Psalms 5:12, 46:1, 138:7-8; Proverbs 3:4-6, 6:16-19, 12:19, 22; Isaiah 54:17; Luke 12:11-12; Acts 11:18; 2 Corinthians 10:5; Ephesians 6:10; 1 Peter 5:7; 1 John 1:9.

Revival

Father God, because You care for Your people and want all mankind to have life, You desire revival. Your revival brings life and nourishment, preservation and restoration. Thank You for sending Jesus to give us Your abundant life.

LORD, start revival in me first. I am Your servant and I place myself in position to receive. I feed on the Scriptures as a sheep feeds in green pastures because Your words are life to me. Holy Spirit of God, You raised Jesus from the dead and You dwell in me. So, I yield to You to energize my spirit, restore my soul and rejuvenate my mortal body. I renew my mind with Your WORD. In my innermost being is a well of living water and I am revived!

Revival not only is life to me, but life to everyone who calls on the Name of The LORD. Therefore, I intercede on behalf of the people. I call upon You as the God of Abraham, Isaac and Jacob. I call upon the mighty Name of Jesus. All mankind needs life, LORD! All mankind needs revival because it is life—Your life. I speak and sow seeds of revival everywhere I go. I send forth angels to reap the harvest of revival all over the world. I put my hand to the sickle to reap the rich harvest of revival in my home, my church, my community, in the marketplace, on the job, in my country and in all the world. Pour Yourself out on the people. Lord of the harvest, send forth laborers, positioning them in strategic places to minister as You pour out Your Spirit on all flesh. Almighty God, show Yourself mighty and strong with signs and wonders. Holy Spirit, breathe on all the people of the world. I pray this in the Name above all names, Jesus. Amen.

Scripture References: John 10:10; Romans 8:11; John 7:38; Psalm 85:6; Matthew 9:38; Romans 12:2.

The U.S. Government

Father, I bring the needs of our government before You and ask You to bless our nation through godly leaders. I magnify the Name of Jesus and declare that He is LORD over this nation.

Father, I pray according to 1 Timothy 2:1-3 which says, "I exhort therefore, that, first of all, supplications, prayers, intercessions, and giving of thanks, be made for all men; for kings, and for all that are in authority; that we may lead a quiet and peaceable life in all godliness and honesty. For this is good and acceptable in the sight of God our Saviour."

I pray, in the Name of The LORD Jesus, for our president, vice president, and all members of the Cabinet, the chief justice and associate justices of the Supreme Court to receive the wisdom of God, to act in obedience to that wisdom and for the power of God to flow in their lives.

I pray for the members of the Senate and the House of Representatives to find Your peace and direction, and for these men and women to act and lead according to Your WORD. A house divided against itself cannot stand, therefore I pray for them to be unified in righteousness for the sake of the nation.

I pray for Your protection to cover all our law enforcement officers and the men and women of the military. I ask for godly counsel and wisdom for judges across this land. In the Name of Jesus, I pray that You and Your kingdom of righteousness be manifested in the hearts of all those who are in authority in any way.

Father, Your WORD says to pray for the peace of Jerusalem because those who love Jerusalem shall prosper. Lord Jesus, because You love Jerusalem and wept over it, I love it also. I pray for Jerusalem to receive the *shalom* of God, which brings wholeness— nothing missing, nothing broken. I pray that no leader of our nation will make any decision that will harm Jerusalem in any way. And in the Name of Jesus, I pray that You reveal Your perfect will to all the leaders of Israel. I ask You, LORD, to reveal Yourself to each person. Thank You, Father, for hearing my prayers that are in accordance with Your will. I receive the answers, in Jesus' Name. Amen.

Scripture References: 1 Timothy 2:1-3; Psalm 122:6; Mark 3:25; Proverbs 21:1; 1 John 5:14-15.

Any Government

Father, in Jesus' Name, I give thanks for our country and its government. I hold up in prayer before You the men and women in positions of authority. I pray for all people in authority over us in any way. I pray that the Spirit of The LORD rests upon them.

I believe that skillful and godly wisdom has entered into the hearts of our leaders and knowledge is pleasant to them. Discretion watches over them; understanding keeps them and delivers them from the way of evil and from evil men.

Your WORD declares that "blessed is the nation whose God is The LORD." I receive Your blessing and declare with my mouth that Your people dwell safely in this land and that they prosper abundantly.

It is written in Your WORD that the heart of the king is in the hand of The LORD and that You turn it whichever way You desire. I believe the heart of our leader is in Your hand and that his decisions are divinely directed by You.

I give thanks to You that the good news of the gospel is published in our land. The WORD of The LORD prevails and grows mightily in the hearts and lives of the people. I give thanks for this land and the leaders You have given to us, in Jesus' Name.

I proclaim that Jesus is LORD over my country.

Scripture References: 1 Timothy 2:1-2; Proverbs 2:11-12; *The Amplified Bible:* Psalm 33:12; Proverbs 21:1. Also see Jeremiah 1:12.

The Nations

O God in heaven, I come before You in the Name of Jesus on behalf of the leaders of (name the nation). First of all, in accordance with 1 Timothy 2:1-2, I intercede and give thanks for all men, for kings and all in authority and expect to live a quiet and peaceable life. I pray for The WORD of God to be given free course and Your people to be delivered from unreasonable and wicked men (2 Thessalonians 3:1-2). The heart of the king is in Your hand and You will turn it whichever way You choose (Proverbs 21:1). I ask You to direct the heart and mind of (name the nation's leader) to make decisions that will lead the country in Your ways and according to Your WORD.

I thank You, LORD, for bringing change to the politics of (name the nation). Thank You for changing the voices of influence to speak in agreement with Your WORD. I ask You to send laborers filled with the spirit of wisdom and might, to surround the leaders of (name the nation) with godly counsel and insight. I also ask You to remove from positions of authority those who stubbornly oppose righteousness, and replace them with men and women who will follow You and Your appointed course for (name the nation).

As we enter the final hours of the last days, I ask for the spirit of faith, the workings of miracles, for signs, wonders, gifts and demonstrations of the Holy Spirit and power to be in strong operation. Let believers in (name the nation) and in every land be unified to stand strong by faith in Jesus, the Anointed One and His Anointing, that Your glory may be revealed in all the earth.

Thank You, Lord, that these requests come to pass. I believe I receive. Amen.

Scripture References: Proverbs 3:3-5; Revelation 3:8; Psalm 5:12; Romans 13:8; 1Thessalonians 4:11-12; 2 Corinthians 9:8, *The Amplified Bible;* Philippians 4:6-7, *The Amplified Bible;* 2 Corinthians 1:3, *The Amplified Bible;* Philippians 4:19.

For Those Who Spread the Gospel

Father, in the Name of Jesus, I pray and confess that the Spirit of The LORD rests upon _____ with the spirit of wisdom and understanding, the spirit of knowledge, and the fear of The LORD. I pray that as Your Spirit rests upon _____, it will make him/her of quick understanding because You, LORD, have anointed and qualified him/her to preach the gospel to the meek, the poor, the wealthy and the afflicted. You have sent _____ to bind up the brokenhearted, to proclaim liberty to the physical and spiritual captives, and to open the prisons and the eyes of those who are bound. All people shall declare that _____ is a minister of The LORD because of The WORD which he/she speaks in power and demonstration of the Holy Spirit.

I pray and believe that no weapon formed against _____ shall prosper and that every tongue that rises against him/her in judgment shall be shown to be in the wrong. I pray that You prosper _____ spiritually, mentally, physically, financially and socially and in all abundance. I confess that _____ holds fast and follows the pattern of wholesome and sound teaching in all faith and love which is for us in Christ Jesus, and that _____ guards and keeps with the greatest care the precious truth which has been entrusted to him/her by the Holy Spirit who makes His home in _____. Lord, I believe and say that You grant unto _____ that with freedom of utterance he/she will open his/her mouth boldly and courageously as he/she ought to do to proclaim the gospel to the people. I hereby confess that I stand behind _____ and undergird him/her in prayer. I will say only good things that will edify _____. I will continue to intercede for him/her and speak and pray blessings upon him/her in the Name of Jesus.

Scripture References: Isaiah 11:2-3, 61:1, 6, 54:17; 2 Timothy 1:13-14, *The Amplified Bible;* Ephesians 6:19, 4:29.

Appendix C
Prayer for Our Partnership
by Kenneth Copeland

Gloria and I pray for you daily, and earnestly believe God that you will prosper and be in health, even as your soul prospers (3 John 2).

In turn, we depend on your prayers of agreement and faith, also.

For that reason, I want you to have the same scripture promises and prayers that I pray for you every day so you can know and agree with me in faith about these things.

As you pray these scriptures, personalize them with your name by simply inserting it in the verses (the first line of each prayer is done for you). Pray the same way for Gloria and me, and anyone else for whom you are standing in faith. Deuteronomy 11:21 will be the result: "That your days may be multiplied, and the days of your children, in the land which The LORD sware unto your fathers to give them, as the days of heaven upon the earth."

Psalm 23

- The LORD is _____ shepherd; _____ shall not want.
- He maketh me to lie down in green pastures: he leadeth me beside the still waters.
- He restoreth my soul: he leadeth me in the paths of righteousness for his name's sake.
- Yea, though I walk through the valley of the shadow of death, I will fear no evil: for thou art with me; thy rod and thy staff they comfort me.
- Thou preparest a table before me in the presence of mine enemies: thou anointest my head with oil; my cup runneth over.
- Surely goodness and mercy shall follow me all the days of my life: and I will dwell in the house of The LORD for ever.

Father, I pray that _____ never have a want unfulfilled. We will follow the Great Shepherd, Jesus, to our green pastures of rest and peace. We will live alongside still waters of abundance and prosperity.

I pray for every Partner who is going through the valley of the shadow of death. We stand together fearlessly and boldly on Your WORD. We come to the table of provision by the blood of Jesus.

Psalm 91

Father, I pray that _____ dwell(s) in the secret place of the Most High. _____ say(s) of The LORD:

- He is my refuge and my fortress: my God; in him will I trust:
- Surely he shall deliver thee from the snare of the fowler, and from the noisome pestilence.
- He shall cover thee with his feathers, and under his wings shalt thou trust: his truth shall be thy shield and buckler.
- Thou shalt not be afraid for the terror by night; nor for the arrow that flieth by day;
- Nor for the pestilence that walketh in darkness; nor for the destruction that wasteth at noonday.
- A thousand shall fall at thy side, and ten thousand at thy right hand; but it shall not come nigh thee.
- Only with thine eyes shalt thou behold and see the reward of the wicked.
- Because thou hast made The LORD, which is my refuge, even the most High, thy habitation;
- There shall no evil befall thee, neither shall any plague come nigh thy dwelling.
- For he shall give his angels charge over thee, to keep thee in all thy ways.

- They shall bear thee up in their hands, lest thou dash thy foot against a stone.
- Thou shalt tread upon the lion and adder: the young lion and the dragon shalt thou trample under feet.
- Because he hath set his love upon me, therefore will I deliver him: I will set him on high, because he hath known my name.
- We shall call upon me, and I will answer him: I will be with him in trouble; I will deliver him, and honour him.
- With long life will I satisfy him, and show him my salvation.

Psalm 103

Father, I pray that _____ walk(s) in all the blessings of our redemption. We exalt and thank You, LORD, saying:

- Bless The LORD, O my soul: and all that is within me, bless his holy name.
- Bless The LORD, O my soul, and forget not all his benefits:
- Who forgiveth all our iniquities; who healeth all our diseases;
- Who redeemeth thy life from destruction; who crowneth us with lovingkindness and tender mercies;
- Who satisfieth thy mouth with good things; so that our youth is renewed like the eagle's.
- The LORD executeth righteousness and judgment for all that are oppressed.
- He made known his ways unto Moses, his acts unto the children of Israel.
- The LORD is merciful and gracious, slow to anger, and plenteous in mercy.
- He will not always chide: neither will he keep his anger for ever.
- He hath not dealt with us after our sins; nor rewarded us according to our iniquities.
- For as the heaven is high above the earth, so great is his mercy toward them that fear him.
- As far as the east is from the west, so far hath he removed our transgressions from us.
- Like as a father pitieth his children, so The LORD pitieth them that fear him.
- For he knoweth our frame; he remembereth that we are dust.
- As for man, his days are as grass: as a flower of the field, so he flourisheth.
- For the wind passeth over it, and it is gone; and the place thereof shall know it no more.
- But the mercy of The LORD is from everlasting to everlasting upon them that fear him, and his righteousness unto children's children;
- To such as keep his covenant, and to those that remember his commandments to do them.
- The LORD hath prepared his throne in the heavens; and his kingdom ruleth over all.
- Bless The LORD, ye his angels, that excel in strength, that do his commandments, hearkening unto the voice of His WORD.
- Bless ye The LORD, all ye his hosts; ye ministers of his, that do his pleasure.
- Bless The LORD, all his works in all places of his dominion: bless The LORD, O my soul.

Isaiah 54

Father, because of what Jesus did for us in Isaiah 53, _____ sing(s) and shout(s) Isaiah 54:

- Sing, O barren, thou that didst not bear; break forth into singing, and cry aloud, thou that didst not travail with child: for more are the children of the desolate than the children of the married wife, saith The LORD.
- Enlarge the place of thy tent, and let them stretch forth the curtains of thine habitations: spare not, lengthen thy cords, and strengthen thy stakes;
- For thou shalt break forth on the right hand and on the left; and thy seed shall inherit the

- Gentiles and make the desolate cities to be inhabited.
- Fear not; for thou shalt not be ashamed: neither be thou confounded; for thou shalt not be put to shame: for thou shalt forget the shame of thy youth, and shalt not remember the reproach of thy widowhood any more.
- For thy Maker is thine husband; The LORD of hosts is his name; and thy Redeemer the Holy One of Israel; the God of the whole earth shall he be called.
- For The LORD hath called thee as a woman forsaken and grieved in spirit, and a wife of youth, when thou wast refused, saith thy God.
- For a small moment have I forsaken thee; but with great mercies will I gather thee.
- In a little wrath I hid my face from thee for a moment; but with everlasting kindness will I have mercy on thee, saith The LORD thy Redeemer.
- For this is as the waters of Noah unto me: for as I have sworn that the waters of Noah should no more go over the earth; so have I sworn that I would not be wroth with thee, nor rebuke thee.
- For the mountains shall depart, and the hills be removed; but my kindness shall not depart from thee, neither shall the covenant of my peace be removed, saith The LORD that hath mercy on thee.
- O thou afflicted, tossed with tempest, and not comforted, behold, I will lay thy stones with fair colours, and lay thy foundations with sapphires.
- And I will make thy windows of agates, and thy gates of carbuncles, and all thy borders of pleasant stones.
- And all thy children shall be taught of The LORD; and great shall be the peace of thy children.
- In righteousness shalt thou be established: thou shalt be far from oppression; for thou shalt not fear: and from terror; for it shall not come near thee.
- Behold, they shall surely gather together, but not by me: whosoever shall gather together against thee shall fall for thy sake.
- Behold, I have created the smith that bloweth the coals in the fire, and that bringeth forth an instrument for his work; and I have created the waster to destroy.
- No weapon that is formed against thee shall prosper; and every tongue that shall rise against thee in judgment thou shalt condemn. This is the heritage of the servants of The LORD, and their righteousness is of me, saith The LORD.

Now, Lord, I pray these powerful, Holy Spirit prayers in the New Testament:

Ephesians 1:16-23

- I cease not to give thanks for _____ making mention of _____ in my prayers;
- That the God of our LORD Jesus Christ, the Father of glory, may give unto you the spirit of wisdom and revelation in the knowledge of him:
- The eyes of your understanding being enlightened; that ye may know what is the hope of his calling, and what the riches of the glory of his inheritance in the saints,
- And what is the exceeding greatness of his power to us-ward who believe, according to the working of his mighty power,
- Which he wrought in Christ, when he raised him from the dead, and set him at his own right hand in the heavenly places,
- Far above all principality, and power, and might, and dominion, and every name that is named, not only in this world, but also in that which is to come:
- And hath put all things under his feet, and gave him to be the head over all things to the church,

- Which is his body, the fulness of him that filleth all in all.

Ephesians 3:14-20

Also, Father, I pray Ephesians 3:14-20:

- For this cause I bow my knees unto the Father of our Lord Jesus Christ,
- Of whom the whole family in heaven and earth is named,
- That he would grant _____, according to the riches of his glory, to be strengthened with might by his Spirit in the inner man;
- That Christ may dwell in your hearts by faith; that ye, being rooted and grounded in love,
- May be able to comprehend with all saints what is the breadth, and length, and depth, and height;
- And to know the love of Christ, which passeth knowledge, that ye might be filled with all the fulness of God.
- Now unto him that is able to do exceeding abundantly above all that we ask or think, according to the power that worketh in us.

Colossians 1:9-11

I pray Colossians 1:9-11:

- For this cause I also, since the day I heard it, do not cease to pray for _____, and to desire that _____ might be filled with the knowledge of his will in all wisdom and spiritual understanding;
- That ye might walk worthy of The LORD unto all pleasing, being fruitful in every good work, and increasing in the knowledge of God;
- Strengthened with all might, according to his glorious power, unto all patience and longsuffering with joyfulness.

1 Thessalonians 5:23

I pray 1 Thessalonians 5:23, that the very God of peace sanctify _____ wholly; and I pray God _____ whole spirit and soul and body be preserved blameless unto the coming of our Lord Jesus Christ.

Mark 16:7-20; Matthew 18:18; Ephesians 4:27

Now, LORD, I plead the blood of Jesus over _____ for protection against every evil spirit, every evil person, every evil thing and every evil plan of the devil. I bind you, Satan, according to The WORD of God.

It is written: "In my name…cast out devils" (Mark 16:17). It is also written: "Whatsoever ye shall bind on earth shall be bound in heaven: and whatsoever ye shall loose on earth shall be loosed in heaven." (Matthew 18:18). So, in the Name of Jesus, Satan, I break your grip, and loose you from _____ and all that is ours.

It is written: "Neither give place to the devil" (Ephesians 4:27). So I take from you, Devil, any place you think you have in our lives. Take your hands off us, NOW! You have no place, in the Name of Jesus!

I John 4:4; 5:1, 4, 18

It is written: "Ye are of God, little children, and have overcome them: because greater is he that is in you, than he that is in the world" (1 John 4:4).

_____ overcome(s) you, Satan, and all your work by the blood of the Lamb and The WORD of our testimony. Our testimony is 1 John 5:1: "Whosoever believeth that Jesus is the Christ is born of God: and every one that loveth him that begat loveth him also that is begotten of him." We believe that!

1 John 5:4 says, "For whatsoever is born of God overcometh the world: and this is the victory that overcometh the world, even our faith." Together, we are world overcomers. Now!

1 John 5:18 says, "We know that whosoever is born of God sinneth not; but he that is begotten of God keepeth himself, and that wicked one toucheth him not." We are born of God, Satan, therefore the seed of sin is not in us. The seed of righteousness is in us. You touch us not! We plead the blood of Jesus!

Now, Father, I pray for _____ according to the full wisdom, will and knowledge of God. I pray in the spirit according to 1 Corinthians 2:7: "But we speak the wisdom of God in a mystery, even the hidden wisdom, which God ordained before the world unto our glory."

_____ stand(s) together in this calling to take The WORD of faith to all the world. We'll preach it without compromise from the top of the world to the bottom and all the way around. Father, reveal to each of us our part of this. What must we do? What must we pray? What must we sow? Together in faith, we can do anything You want us to do. We can do all things through the anointing which strengthens us!

You are truly special to Gloria and me, and to all of us at KCM and Eagle Mountain International Church. We are Partners in all of this.

Take the time to pray these scriptures every day. These words will be a springboard in the spirit that will lead you into areas of prayer you've never experienced before. Amen!

Appendix D
Prayer of Agreement Checklist
by Kenneth Copeland

The prayer of agreement is one of the most powerful tools God has given us. It is a prayer that Jesus Himself guaranteed would bring results every time: "If two of you agree on earth about anything that they may ask," He said, "it shall be done for them by My Father who is in heaven" (Matthew 18:19, *NAS*).

When you don't see the results He promised, the problem usually lies in one of four areas.

Run a harmony check.

The word *agree* that Jesus uses in Matthew 18:19 can also be translated "to harmonize" or "to make a symphony." A symphony is composed of many instruments, which, when played together, seem to be a single voice.

If you've ever heard a symphony, you know that when the individual instruments are tuning up, each one playing separately, it's not much to listen to. But when the conductor raises his baton and all those instruments begin to harmonize, the sound they make is tremendously powerful.

The same is true in prayer. Believers agreeing together in the Holy Spirit are a powerful, unstoppable force. That's why Satan fights Christian families. That's why he doesn't want men and women unified in marriage. He wants us fighting and fussing all the time because he knows it will hinder our prayers (see 1 Peter 3:7).

Anytime you fail to get results from the prayer of agreement, run a harmony check. Ask the Holy Spirit to show you if you're in strife with your spouse (or anyone else). Then follow the instructions in Mark 11:25, where Jesus tells us, "When ye stand praying, forgive, if ye have aught against any: that your Father also which is in heaven may forgive you."

It is not sufficient for you and your spouse to simply agree on the particular issue you are praying about. You must also be in harmony in other areas as well. So make a harmony check!

Establish your heart on God's WORD.

The prayer of agreement will only work if it is based on The WORD of God. You and your wife might jump up one day and agree that you'll own a hundred oil wells by midnight, but you'll never see that prayer of agreement come to pass, because it's not founded on The WORD of God.

So go to The WORD first. Find the promise that covers the particular situation you're praying about. Then write it down and meditate on it until, as Psalm 112:7 says, your "heart is fixed, trusting in The LORD."

Fix your mind on The WORD.

Second Corinthians 10:5 tells us to bring "into captivity every thought to the obedience of Christ." You must do that if you're to see results from your prayers of agreement. Do what the Bible says and "think on these things" (Philippians 4:8). What things? Things from The WORD of God!

Say to yourself, "I'll not think on anything contrary to this agreement." Then, when Satan tries to slip in negative thoughts and break down your faith, you'll have to tell him, "No, no, no, Devil! I don't believe what you say. I believe what The WORD says."

Then, get out your Bible. Go back to The WORD and soak your mind in it. Obey Proverbs 4:21 and "keep it before your eyes."

Act as if it's done.

This is where so many believers miss it. They pray the prayer of agreement, taking a faith stand together. Then as soon as they walk out of the prayer closet, they start wringing their hands and saying, "Oh my, I just don't know what we're going to do if this problem doesn't get solved!"

Don't make that mistake. Once you've settled the issue through the prayer of agreement, refuse to act as though that issue is a problem anymore. Instead, just start praising God. In every way you can, act as though all is well.

When people ask you about the matter, just answer them with faith. Say, "Glory to God, that issue is handled. My spouse and I have agreed in prayer. God is honoring our agreement. And as far as we're concerned, that problem is behind us."

The prayer of agreement is a powerful tool. So don't be discouraged by your past experience. Just make the necessary adjustments, and keep on in agreement. Run a harmony check. Establish your heart on The WORD. Fix your mind on The WORD. Act as if it's done. And anything you ask shall be done for you by your Father in heaven.

Appendix E
Take Time to Pray

Prophecy delivered by

Kenneth Copeland at the

1986 Dallas Victory Campaign

Spend the time to pray. When you're firmly convinced of My will, take time to pray. When you're not convinced, and you don't know just exactly which way things are going, take time to pray. Don't be caught without prayer.

If you remember, in My WORD I said to My disciples, "This kind cometh not out but by prayer and fasting." But I didn't go off and pray and fast before I ministered to that young man. No, you see, I had already prayed, I had already fasted. You be that way. You be instant in season and out of season, ready with a word that's seasoned with salt. The only way you can be that way is to have an energetic, solid, WORD-based prayer life.

Spend time with Me, saith The LORD. Listen to My Spirit. There will be days ahead when things look like it's awfully quiet. It looks like the Spirit of God is not moving very much. Don't run and jump into things and try to stir up something when you have no anointing to do so. And you won't know whether you're anointed to or not anointed to if you don't take time to pray, seek the face of The LORD and pray in tongues.

Pray in tongues. Pray in the spirit. Not only just your hour a day that surely you spend praying in tongues, but all during the day, all during the day, even when it's under your breath or like you say, "to yourself," because I'm in your self. I'll hear you in your self because I'm in your self and you're in My self. We are one Spirit, saith The LORD. You can spend time all day long communicating with Me in the spirit. For a very precious time is coming.

A very outstanding time is on the way. A time is coming when there will be a manifestation of angels more than usual, more than what there has been in the past. Many of you are going to witness for yourselves the angel that has been put in charge and in command of your ministry and your life. Many of you are going to have visitations from the spirit realm. Many of you will have divinely appointed visions and dreams. Well, don't get all puffed up about it and say, "Boy, I must be really something. Look what God's doing for me." No, you're just part of the times.

It's time for these things to happen, saith The LORD. It's time for spiritual activity to increase. Oh, yes, demonic activity will increase along at the same time. But don't let that disturb you.

Don't be disturbed when people accuse you of thinking you're God. Don't be disturbed when people accuse you of a fanatical way of life. Don't be disturbed when people put you down and speak harshly and roughly of you. They spoke that way of Me, should they not speak that way of you?

The more you get to be like Me, the more they're going to think that way of you. They crucified Me for claiming that I was God. But I didn't claim I was God; I just claimed I walked with Him and that He was in Me. Hallelujah. That's what you're doing.

No, you don't think you're God, you just know you're the family of God. And you've begun to act like God. You've begun to realize He that's within you is greater than he that is in the world. And I'll tell you right now, saith The LORD of Grace, your LORD and Savior, your soon-coming King, I'll tell you right now, it gives Me great pleasure when you try to act like Me. It gives Me great pleasure when you try to speak like Me. It gives Me great pleasure. It even gives Me pleasure when I hear those inspired by the devil rise up and begin to chatter about you and to patter about you like little monkeys.

No, not because they're coming against you but because I know the time is near. I know the end is close. I know it won't be but hours until you and I, face to face, will be able to share great things of great joy as we enter together into the presence of the Holy Father.

I love you, saith The LORD. I care for you. But you're My choice. You're My leaders. I'm going to send you places you didn't think you were qualified to go. I'm going to send you places that are going to be so tough you'll wish you were God when you get there. You're going to call on your God. And there will be those who smile and say, "He knows his God."

But you're My best. And I don't save the best in reserve. I put the best on the front line. You're My best. You're My troops. You've learned a little about your armor. You've learned a little about your faith. You've learned a little about My ways that are higher than your ways. And I must take advantage of what you've learned and put you up on the front line.

You'll be My singers in front of the army. You'll be My praisers out where there is no praise. You'll take My WORD into places in the earth where My voice is little heard and My light very, very dim.

You'll speak My Name into the ear of people who have never heard My Name. And when you do, I will work with and confirm The WORD of your lips with signs following. Great and great and great and then greater and greater and greater and greater shall be the manifestations of My Spirit.

Don't get disturbed because it's not happening just like you thought it was going to. My strategy is right. I know My business, saith The LORD. I am moving in ways right now that you don't know of. The lights will come together all over the world, a light in this country connecting with a prayer light of a person in another country.

Oh, there's no time nor distance in the spirit realm. You'll be connected together at times like you've never witnessed before. Suddenly, you'll be standing in that country, and suddenly you'll deliver a message, and then suddenly you'll be right back in your kitchen again. Oh, I have some outstanding things, saith The LORD.

So just stay steady. Stay steady on The WORD. Stay steady in prayer. Stay steady in praise, and enjoy the Spirit of God. Enjoy your deliverance from what the world is going through, because I am your soon-coming King, saith The LORD Christ. Hallelujah!

Additional Materials to Help You Develop an Effective Prayer Life

By Kenneth Copeland:

- Fasting and Prayer (4-CD series)
- Intercessory Prayer (4-CD series)
- One Word From God Can Change Your Prayer Life (book)
- Prayer Series (45 *BVOV* broadcasts on DVD)
  - #1 Effective Prayer
  - #2 Your Right to Believe
  - #3 Prayer That Changes Things
  - #4 Pressing in for Victory
  - #5 The Power of Intercession
  - #6 The Power of United Prayer
  - #7 The Prayer of Faith
  - #8 Prayer That Brings Results
  - #9 Connecting With God
- Prayer—Your Foundation for Success (book)
- Prayer—Your Path to Every Victory (12-CD series)
- Seven Steps to Prayer That Bring Results (4-CD series)
- The Outpouring of the Holy Spirit—The Result of Prayer (book)

By Terri Copeland Pearsons

- A Deeper Understanding of Praying in the Spirit (6-CD series)
- Letting Him Lead—Following the Holy Spirit in Prayer (3-CD series)
- Praying Out Your Destiny (3-CD series)
- Partnering With the Holy Spirit (single CD)
- Praying With Power (2-CD set)
- Your Place in Prayer (DVD)

Prayer for Salvation and Baptism in the Holy Spirit

Heavenly Father, I come to You in the Name of Jesus. Your Word says, "Whosoever shall call on the name of the Lord shall be saved" (Acts 2:21). I am calling on You. I pray and ask Jesus to come into my heart and be Lord over my life according to Romans 10:9-10: "If thou shalt confess with thy mouth the Lord Jesus, and shalt believe in thine heart that God hath raised him from the dead, thou shalt be saved. For with the heart man believeth unto righteousness; and with the mouth confession is made unto salvation." I do that now. I confess that Jesus is Lord, and I believe in my heart that God raised Him from the dead.

I am now reborn! I am a Christian—a child of Almighty God! I am saved! You also said in Your Word, "If ye then, being evil, know how to give good gifts unto your children: HOW MUCH MORE shall your heavenly Father give the Holy Spirit to them that ask him?" (Luke 11:13). I'm also asking You to fill me with the Holy Spirit. Holy Spirit, rise up within me as I praise God. I fully expect to speak with other tongues as You give me the utterance (Acts 2:4). In Jesus' Name. Amen!

Begin to praise God for filling you with the Holy Spirit. Speak those words and syllables you receive—not in your own language, but the language given to you by the Holy Spirit. You have to use your own voice. God will not force you to speak. Don't be concerned with how it sounds. It is a heavenly language!

Continue with the blessing God has given you and pray in the spirit every day.

You are a born-again, Spirit-filled believer. You'll never be the same!

Find a good church that boldly preaches God's Word and obeys it. Become part of a church family who will love and care for you as you love and care for them.

We need to be connected to each other. It increases our strength in God. It's God's plan for us.

Make it a habit to watch the *Believer's Voice of Victory* television broadcast and become a doer of the Word, who is blessed in his doing (James 1:22-25).

About the Authors

Kenneth and Gloria Copeland are the best-selling authors of more than 60 books. They have also co-authored numerous books including *Family Promises,* the *LifeLine Your 10-Day Spiritual Action Plan* series and *From Faith to Faith—A Daily Guide to Victory.* As founders of Kenneth Copeland Ministries in Fort Worth, Texas, Kenneth and Gloria have been circling the globe with the uncompromised Word of God since 1967, preaching and teaching a lifestyle of victory for every Christian.

Their daily and Sunday *Believer's Voice of Victory* television broadcasts now air on more than 500 stations around the world, and the *Believer's Voice of Victory* magazine is distributed to nearly 600,000 believers worldwide. Kenneth Copeland Ministries' international prison ministry reaches more than 20,000 new inmates every year and receives more than 20,000 pieces of correspondence each month. Their teaching materials can also be found on the World Wide Web. With offices and staff in the United States, Canada, England, Australia, Singapore, South Africa and Ukraine, Kenneth and Gloria's teaching materials—books, magazines, audios and videos—have been translated into at least 26 languages to reach the world with the love of God.

Learn more about Kenneth Copeland Ministries
by visiting our website at **www.kcm.org**

We're Here for You!

Believer's Voice of Victory Television Broadcast

Join Kenneth and Gloria Copeland and the *Believer's Voice of Victory* broadcasts Monday through Friday and on Sunday each week, and learn how faith in God's Word can take your life from ordinary to extraordinary. This teaching from God's Word is designed to get you where you want to be—*on top!*

You can catch the *Believer's Voice of Victory* broadcast on your local, cable or satellite channels.* Also available 24 hours on webcast at BVOV.TV.

* Check your local listings for times and stations in your area.

Believer's Voice of Victory Magazine

Enjoy inspired teaching and encouragement from Kenneth and Gloria Copeland and guest ministers each month in the *Believer's Voice of Victory* magazine. Also included are real-life testimonies of God's miraculous power and divine intervention in the lives of people just like you!

It's more than just a magazine—it's a ministry.

To receive a FREE subscription to
Believer's Voice of Victory, write to:

Kenneth Copeland Ministries
Fort Worth, TX 76192-0001
Or call:
800-600-7395
(7 a.m.-5 p.m. CT)
Or visit our website at:
www.kcm.org

If you are writing from outside the U.S., please contact the KCM office nearest you. Addresses for all Kenneth Copeland Ministries offices are listed on the previous pages.

World Offices
Kenneth Copeland Ministries

For more information about KCM and our products,
please write to the office nearest you:

Kenneth Copeland Ministries
Fort Worth, TX 76192-0001

Kenneth Copeland
Locked Bag 2600
Mansfield Delivery Centre
QUEENSLAND 4122
AUSTRALIA

Kenneth Copeland
Private Bag X 909
FONTAINEBLEAU
2032
REPUBLIC OF SOUTH AFRICA

Kenneth Copeland Ministries
Post Office Box 84
L'VIV 79000
UKRAINE

Kenneth Copeland
Post Office Box 15
BATH
BA1 3XN
U.K.

Kenneth Copeland
PO Box 3111 STN LCD 1
Langley BC V3A 4R3
CANADA

**Kenneth Copeland Ministries
Singapore Ltd.**
Rochor Post Office
Locked Bag Service No. 1
Singapore 911884